RUNNING
CHALLENGES

RUNNING CHALLENGES

100 OF THE BEST RUNS IN ENGLAND, SCOTLAND AND WALES

KERI WALLACE

Vertebrate Publishing, Sheffield
www.adventurebooks.com

RUNNING CHALLENGES

100 OF THE BEST RUNS IN ENGLAND, SCOTLAND AND WALES

First published in 2024 by Vertebrate Publishing.

VERTEBRATE PUBLISHING
Omega Court, 352 Cemetery Road, Sheffield S11 8FT, United Kingdom.
www.adventurebooks.com

A CIP catalogue record for this book is available from the British Library.

ISBN 978-1-83981-085-5 (Paperback)
ISBN 978-1-83981-178-4 (Ebook)

Front cover: South Glen Shiel Ridge (route 61). © Finlay Wild
Back cover: TOP Cumbrian Traverse (route 28), © Kirsty Reade; MIDDLE Ring of Steall (route 53), © Keri Wallace; BOTTOM Corris to Abergynolwyn (route 88), © Rob Johnson

All photography individually credited.

Mapping contains data from OS © Crown copyright and database right (2024) and © OpenStreetMap contributors, *www.openstreetmap.org/copyright*
Relief shading produced from data derived from U.S. Geological Survey, National Geospatial Program.
Cartography by Richard Ross, Active Maps Ltd. *www.activemaps.co.uk*

Cover design, layout and production by Jane Beagley.
www.adventurebooks.com

Printed and bound in Slovenia by Latitude Press.

Vertebrate Publishing is committed to printing on paper from sustainable sources.

© KERI WALLACE

Contents

Introduction . . . . **xi**

Route selection . . . . **xi**

How to use this book . . . . **xii**

Etiquette and style . . . . **xiii**

Make it your own . . . . **xiii**

Mountain safety . . . . **xiv**

Environment and access . . . . **xv**

100 Running Challenges

England (routes 1–34) . . . . **xx**

Scotland (routes 35–70) **54**

Wales (routes 71–100) **118**

Appendix **171**

Acknowledgements **172**

Introduction

Per aspera ad astra – through suffering to the stars

Since the earliest civilisations, mankind has known the value of a struggle – for developing our mental and emotional toughness, for enabling us to come back stronger from setbacks and make meaningful progress. We achieve little success without failures along the way and it is through our hardships that we acquire greatness. In these ways, running is a valuable metaphor for life – in both, there is no growth without challenge.

What is a 'challenge', and why is it so important?

Taking on a challenge means something different to each and every person, but ultimately it involves an effort (often a struggle) which advances us in some way, whether that be physically, emotionally or spiritually. Just as people run for different reasons, we all have different strengths and weaknesses, so choosing or designing a running 'challenge' is a very personal process. For some, it is about chasing a record or a personal best, while for others it might be about exploring a new place or understanding themselves. Some of us are curious about our limits, while others crave solitude or a spiritual journey. Some people chase challenges as a way of raising money for charity while others need these experiences for healing, mental health or well-being in a frantic world. In truth, we often get more than we've bargained for with running challenges, ending up with much of the above rolled into one.

In my experience, I've found that the more you invest personally in a challenge, the more you get out of it – which is a great reason to dream big and push hard! Challenges are important because they involve self-learning and provide a way for us to expand our life experience. Only by doing things that stretch us beyond our familiar comfort zone are we able to push back against our limitations. The more we do this, the bigger our comfort zones become. And who knows what is possible. You simply don't know what you can do – until you give it a try.

The ethos of this book

If somebody gives you an idea for a running challenge, shows you the way and gives you all the important advice you need to complete it, is it a challenge any more? Will it still be rewarding? I believe that much of the intrigue and motivation we derive from running challenges (and ultimately the satisfaction we feel on completing them) comes directly from the time and effort we put into their conception. Researching, planning, training for and orchestrating a big personal challenge is in many ways the essence of the challenge itself. With each failure we learn something new and become more determined to reach our goal. For this reason, this book is not an exhaustive 'how to' guide but rather a source of inspiration; a compilation of ideas. I have deliberately kept detail to a minimum to allow room for you to find out more and to personalise your adventure.

Another way to embed yourself in your chosen running challenge is to find out about its origin and history. Understanding how a challenge came to be and how it has developed over the years helps to foster a connection with the route and to create a respect for those who have gone before, as well as for the trail and the landscape through which it passes.

To get the most out of a running challenge, you need to do the legwork, in more ways than one!

Route selection

Whatever your fitness, ability or background, there is a running challenge out there for you. But something that is a challenge for one person may not be challenging at all for another. For this reason, this book includes a range of routes that will stretch runners from beginners to seasoned mountain athletes. Some of the challenges are recognised trails, rounds or routes with established records or fastest known times (FKTs), but others are simply popular routes that might be considered a rite of passage for developing runners. Often these trails are just examples of many such fine routes across Great Britain and should be seen as a benchmark or entryway into a particular type of trail or fell running route.

The challenges in this book span trail running, fell running and mountain running (with some routes involving easy scrambling sections).

- **Trail running** follows trails or paths which are visible on the map and on the ground (though there may be some sections where the trail is faint or temporarily absent).
- **Fell running** (aka **hill running** in Scotland) follows upland, off-road routes which often avoid (marked) trails and often take a direct line through steep terrain. It regularly involves rough, broken or boggy ground.
- **Mountain running** is technical fell running on high-level mountain terrain. Often including rocky summits, exposure and ridge-running. Sometimes including scrambling – previous scrambling or climbing experience is recommended for routes involving this kind of terrain.

Where a route follows an established ultra-distance 'big trail' (e.g. one of Great Britain's many National Trails), I have chosen to focus on just one section, with the aim of making this book more accessible. Such sections might be the most scenic, popular, wildest or most difficult stretches of the full trail. Runners with longer aspirations could seek to link multiple sections or tackle the full distance.

Some routes included are iconic races (where access is restricted outside of the event) and most routes have races somewhere along their length.

In choosing these 100 routes I have prioritised memorable running over easy logistics. Many of these routes therefore involve personal or public transport to link the start and finish of the challenge – but nothing worth doing ever came easy.

How to use this book

The aim of this book is to provide a loose progression of running challenges which will inspire and direct trail runners towards future possible goals in Great Britain, while helping build the relevant skills and experience along the way.

Challenges are grouped by country and roughly ordered by ascending difficulty, ranging from short, straightforward trails to bucket-list multi-day challenges. It should be noted, however, that 'difficulty' takes many forms and that distance, ascent, terrain and navigational complexity trade off against each other in determining how hard any particular challenge will feel. Difficulty is of course also related to the fitness, experience and skill set of the runner in question. The increasing difficulty in the included routes is therefore not linear and all challenges should be researched fully and appraised with the individual's abilities in mind.

Each of the 100 challenges includes the *distance* (in kilometres) and cumulative total *ascent* (in metres). The *terrain* and level of *navigational skills* required are denoted as follows:

Terrain
Trail running
Fell running
Mountain running

Navigation
1 Fully waymarked/good waymarking
2 Partial waymarking/occasional self-navigation required
3 No waymarking/self-navigation required throughout
4 Difficult self-navigation/complex terrain

Any safety issues relating to each challenge are identified in the text (for example, technical terrain, major road or river crossings, tides or instability/erosion of sea cliffs).

Other useful information is provided for every challenge including a basic map, route profile, start and finish points, and details of public transport and parking.

There are short sections detailing other nearby options which might interest you, any races which use this route and some suggestions for what to tackle next

– these point towards similar challenges elsewhere in Great Britain and can be used to consolidate experience before progressing further down the list or simply to replicate the fun if you find something you really enjoy.

To use this book, simply pick your battle and get researching. Go longer, higher or more technical than you ever have before, or try something new. Make sure you refer to the **Mountain safety** section on page xiv to ensure you have the relevant skills and experience necessary to stay safe.

If you like the sound of a particular challenge but are uncomfortable with an unsupported format, consider the races referenced for each route. These may provide a challenge of similar difficulty but within the structure of an organised event.

Etiquette and style

For some of the more long-standing running challenges there is sometimes an unwritten 'code of conduct' for contenders. Consequently, it is all too easy, especially in this era of social media, to fall foul of criticism about the way a respected challenge is undertaken or the style in which it was completed. For example, many of the oldest fell running challenges have very particular rules about start location, direction of travel or order of summits/checkpoints visited. Some require registration, prohibit professionally guided attempts or have rules about the presence of supporters for verification.

For example, anyone who has previously benefited from the support of their peers in completing one of Great Britain's Big Three mountain rounds (the Bob Graham Round, the Paddy Buckley Round or the Charlie Ramsay Round), is generally expected to reciprocate by offering their support for other runners attempting the challenge in the future. It is also common for the current record holder to form part of the support team for contenders attempting to break their record.

There are also a number of considerations around seasons. Some summer running challenges have winter counterparts with distinct FKTs. 'Winter' is usually defined by the calendar dates December to March but for fell running (especially in Scotland) the presence of 'winter conditions' is often considered a prerequisite.

Time-honoured traditions such as these are part of the rich tapestry of a historic British sport, but ultimately each individual should decide for themselves what their challenge will look like, depending on what they plan to 'claim' and how much 'validation' they seek from their fellow runners. In the end, honesty and transparency are more important than style.

Different styles of undertaking a running challenge:
Supported – undertaken with the assistance of others for pacing, carrying gear, motivation or navigation.
Solo-Supported – undertaken alone but with the assistance of others at a number of support points (for example, for resupply or to change footwear).
Solo-self-supported – undertaken alone but with the benefit of self-arranged stashes or food-drops on route.
Solo-unsupported – undertaken without any assistance (and in purist terms, without making contact with any persons).

Make it your own

I would urge readers to treat this book as a platform from which a personalised adventure can be created. Would you like to take a challenge and make it shorter? Make it longer? Start from elsewhere? Split it over several days or add cafe stops? Maybe you would like to add some swimming, cycling, climbing or simply link things and places that you love.

There are lots of ways to design your own personal running challenge from scratch. Can you run the length of a meaningful boundary-line or traverse an interesting geographical or historical feature? How about linking existing challenges or collecting trig points, tops, beaches, lakes or castles? A personalised running challenge can be more rewarding than simply following in others' footsteps. Who knows, maybe somebody will decide to follow in yours!

Mountain safety

In order to stay safe on running challenges in remote or mountainous terrain, it is essential that you have the right kit and experience for your route. While it might seem laudable to 'jump in' and take on something much longer or bigger than you have ever tried before, this is simply not the case if it involves venturing ill-equipped and inexperienced into locations where Mountain Rescue would need to be called if things went wrong. A good level of autonomy and an understanding of your own abilities is essential for choosing the right running challenge for you.

Weather

Make sure you carry more than enough suitable clothing/layers and anticipate the worst-case scenario in terms of forecasted weather. British mountain weather is notoriously unpredictable and should not be underestimated. It is essential that you know what weather to expect at height on your run (by referring to mountain weather forecasts/charts instead of regular weather forecasts – see page 171 for details).

Be aware of regional differences in weather and seasons across the various mountainous areas in Great Britain. For example, the Scottish Highlands are much colder and snowier in winter than elsewhere and see fewer hours of daylight. Winter conditions in Scotland are severe and often dangerous/unsuitable for standard running equipment and attire. The same can of course be said of all mountainous areas in Great Britain in the winter months, but there is a higher likelihood of 'full winter' conditions further north. For more information on mountain safety in the Scottish winter, visit: *www.mountaineering.scot/safety-and-skills/thinkwinter* It's worth doing a winter skills course with a qualified instructor if you want to run in the mountains in winter – see page 171 for details.

Navigation

Runners should always carry a map and compass, and know how to use them. A smartwatch or handheld GPS device can be useful time-saving tools but overreliance on them is a risk to your safety. There have been many cases of battery or device failures and also human error in their use. Mountain navigation is a very particular skill and needs to be learned and practised ahead of any mountain running challenge, whether independently or on an instructed course (see page 171 for details).

It is important not to just 'blindly follow' a GPX track or other electronic navigational aid in the mountains. Direct lines or unsubstantiated routes may not take steep or technical terrain into account and may lead you into difficulty. Plan and revise (maybe even recce) your routes meticulously ahead of time to make sure you understand the full nature of the challenge. Always have one or two escape routes in mind to shorten your day if things don't go as planned.

Food and drink

Make sure you carry enough food and water with you or have access to drinking water on the route. It is possible to refill your water bottle safely from streams and rivers in high and remote locations. The higher the water source, the safer it will be. Check on the map that there is no human habitation, farmland, bothy, popular wild camping site or other source of anthropogenic pollution upstream of your location. Do not drink from non-running water sources such as tarns or lochans unless you have the facility to boil or purify that water. When filling your bottle or soft flask, look for clear, aerated (i.e. tumbling) running water.

Midges and ticks

Midges can be an annoyance in the summer across Great Britain. The tiny insects don't like any kind of breeze, so you'll generally be OK up in the hills, but you might need repellent if stopping in sheltered or boggy areas, or in very still weather. Midges are most prevalent in Scotland, where it is usual to carry a midge net and repellent in summer.

Ticks, which can spread Lyme disease, are found across Great Britain in the summer months. Be aware of the risks, carry a tick remover and check yourself at the end of the day. Seek medical advice if you are bitten and then develop a 'bullseye' reaction at the bite spot. *www.lymediseaseaction.org.uk*

River crossings

Think ahead and identify any large river crossings on your route. River levels can change rapidly in the mountains following heavy rainfall, snow thaw and – occasionally – dam release. Know how to identify when a river is acceptable to cross and how to do this safely. Make sure you plan an alternative route in advance, and if at all in doubt, use it.

Technical terrain

It is important to know what to expect of the graded technical terrain which features in some of the routes included in this book (grade 1–3 scrambling – for explanations of the different scrambling grades, see: *www.thebmc.co.uk/understanding-scrambling-grades*). The ability to move safely and confidently on this kind of ground is essential and should be gained through progressive experience and/or professional instruction outside any running challenge. Previous experience, a head for heights and an aptitude for exposed terrain is necessary for any of the mountain running challenges in this book. If you are at all unsure, consider hiring a professional guide to recce the technical sections or to try your hand at a similar objective without the more technical terrain.

Rescue

Always notify someone of your plans and expected schedule before you start. In the event of an accident or emergency call **999** (or **112**) and ask for **POLICE** and then **MOUNTAIN RESCUE**.

In locations where your phone signal is poor or absent it is sometimes possible to send an emergency SMS if you have pre-registered your phone with *www.emergencysms.net*

In the absence of any phone signal, you should blow a whistle to attract attention, using six consecutive blasts, repeated once a minute. If running solo, you might also consider carrying a personal locator beacon for its emergency SOS function or using a tracker to keep friends or family updated on your progress.

Mountain Rescue teams in Great Britain are comprised of unpaid volunteers, so self-rescue should be attempted if at all possible. You are more likely to be able to do this if you carry running poles (useful for hobbling back to safety following a strain or sprain) and a suitable first aid kit. Always protect your mobile phone and conserve battery life wherever possible.

Environment and access

As responsible outdoor enthusiasts it is important that we minimise our impact on the environment we run through. Best practice includes sticking to the main trail where possible and avoiding shortcuts in popular areas where maintained trails are provided (for example, don't cut the corners off a zigzagging trail). This is to reduce surrounding soil erosion and prevent the gradual formation of duplicate trails across the landscape. Consider limiting the number of pacers/supporters running with you on popular mountain routes such as the Bob Graham Round where the footfall of runners contributes to significant erosion of the trails. Along coastal paths, follow signed diversions and stick to the main trails to reduce further erosion.

Leave only footprints wherever you run. Take all litter home with you and remember that even some biodegradable waste (such as banana skins or orange peel) takes a very long time to decompose in a mountain environment and is unsightly for others. Pay particular attention when pulling kit out of vest pockets or using energy gels on the go – it is all too easy to lose wrappers to the wind without realising it. Store used gel wrappers securely in your vest where they won't escape. You might even consider 'plogging' on your training runs (collecting litter as you go) and leaving the trails better than you found them.

If your running challenge involves overnighting in refuges, howfs or bothies, make sure you follow the Bothy Code: *www.mountainbothies.org.uk* If bivvying or wild camping, leave no trace. Do not make or cause any fires anywhere in the landscape (avoid moving rocks for fire-pits, damaging trees for firewood or burning fragile upland soils and vegetation). Burned logs and fire debris are unsightly and scorched ground takes years to recover. Instead use a camping stove which does not transfer heat to the ground. Only wild camp where permitted to do so.

In remote locations, where there is no access to toilet facilities, make sure that you find somewhere away from the trail and dig a hole 15 centimetres deep. This should be somewhere at least 30 metres away from water and not in a place that others might use (for example, climbers, wild campers or exploring children). If you use toilet paper, burn it or take it away with you – don't bury it or leave it under rocks. In popular areas where such a location is not available, double-bag your waste and carry it out with you. The same applies for all sanitary products.

The regulations around land access vary across Great Britain – the following tips and resources should help:

- Respect access restrictions and understand which areas are Open Access Land in England and Wales:
  www.gov.uk/right-of-way-open-access-land
  www.naturalresources.wales/days-out/places-to-visit
- Always follow the Countryside Code:
  www.gov.uk/government/publications/the-countryside-code
- In Scotland, where runners have a right to responsible access, ensure you follow the Scottish Outdoor Access Code:
  www.outdooraccess-scotland.scot

Close gates behind you and do not climb drystone walls or bend wire fences. If you run with a dog, be mindful of livestock and wildlife. You might even consider supporting the organisations and charities that maintain the trails and who lobby for access on your behalf in the areas that you use.

In Scotland, minimise disturbance during the stag stalking season (1 July to 20 October) and the hind stalking season (21 October to 15 February) by seeking information on where stalking might be taking place. In the central and eastern Highlands, the grouse shooting season runs from 12 August to 10 December. Find out if a shoot is happening anywhere along your route and plan a diversion or wait until after the shoot has taken place and it is safe to cross. Details about stalking and shooting practices are available at: *www.outdooraccess-scotland.scot*

As runners we should also play our part in addressing the wider global climate crisis. Where possible take public transport, lift-share or use another form of human-powered transport such as a bike to link the start and finish of linear challenges. Reduce waste and purchase from sustainable brands where possible. It also helps to 'shop local' and generally support the local rural economy in the places that you visit.

This book focuses on running challenges in Great Britain to encourage runners to look closer to home for their next adventure or bucket-list aspiration. Our landscape is highly varied, with a rich diversity of natural and cultural heritage – it's simply a brilliant playground! Limiting global air travel will help reduce carbon emissions and contribute towards a more environmentally responsible running community.

ENGLAND

01 **Whinlatter Forest Parkrun**
5km | TRAIL | NAVIGATION **1**

02 **Hampstead Heath**
10km | TRAIL | NAVIGATION **2**

03 **Brown Willy**
9km | TRAIL | NAVIGATION **3**

04 **Cat Bells**
6km | TRAIL | NAVIGATION **3**

05 **Pendle Hill**
8km | TRAIL | NAVIGATION **2**

06 **Avebury to Ogbourne St George**
15km | TRAIL | NAVIGATION **1**

07 **Westhumble to Merstham**
17km | TRAIL | NAVIGATION **1**

08 **Helvellyn Edges**
14km | FELL | NAVIGATION **3**

09 **Isle of Portland**
20km | TRAIL | NAVIGATION **1**

10 **Nine Standards Rigg**
19km | FELL | NAVIGATION **4**

11 **Malvern Hills**
20km | TRAIL | NAVIGATION **2**

12 **Beachy Head and the Seven Sisters**
24km | TRAIL | NAVIGATION **2**

13 **Coledale Horseshoe**
15km | FELL | NAVIGATION **3**

14 **Sheringham to Sea Palling**
37km | TRAIL | NAVIGATION **1**

15 **Middleton-in-Teesdale to Dufton**
33km | FELL | NAVIGATION **1**

16 **Chollerford to Greenhead**
31km | TRAIL | NAVIGATION **1**

17 **Edale Skyline**
33km | FELL | NAVIGATION **4**

18 **Howgill Fells**
21km | FELL | NAVIGATION **4**

19 **Nine Edges**
36km | FELL | NAVIGATION **3**

20 **Chevy Chase**
31km | FELL | NAVIGATION **4**

21 **Sennen Cove to St Ives**
37km | TRAIL | NAVIGATION **1**

22 **Langdale Skyline**
32km | MOUNTAIN | NAVIGATION **4**

23 **Yorkshire Three Peaks**
39km | TRAIL | NAVIGATION **2**

24 **Chagford to Ivybridge**
50km | TRAIL | NAVIGATION **1**

25 **Derwent Watershed**
69km | FELL | NAVIGATION **4**

26 **George Fisher's Tea Round**
47km | FELL | NAVIGATION **4**

27 **Old County Tops Fell Race**
57km | FELL | NAVIGATION **4**

28 **Cumbrian Traverse**
50km | FELL | NAVIGATION **4**

29 **Bay Limestone Round**
90km | TRAIL | NAVIGATION **4**

30 **Gerry Charnley Round**
62km | FELL | NAVIGATION **4**

31 **Hardmoors 55**
86km | FELL | NAVIGATION **1**

32 **The Fellsman**
97km | FELL | NAVIGATION **4**

33 **Bob Graham Round**
103km | FELL | NAVIGATION **4**

34 **Offroad JOGLE**
over 1,400km | TRAIL | NAVIGATION **3**

01

WHINLATTER FOREST PARKRUN

5km | TRAIL | NAVIGATION 1 fully waymarked
LAKE DISTRICT

A hilly run through Whinlatter Forest Park taking in beautiful views of Derwent Water and the surrounding mountain ranges.

Dubbed 'Beauty and the Beast', this is a challenging point-to-point route with an additional mini-loop at the top. The course belongs to Forestry England and is used by parkrun on Saturday mornings. The route is permanently waymarked and anyone visiting the forest can enjoy this short trail by following the pink running signs.

Whinlatter is most famous for its mountain biking trails, but the site also offers Segway and Go Ape along with Gruffalo sculptures and a Wildplay trail for families.

OTHER OPTIONS There are a number of short waymarked 'walking' trails in the park, as well as a waymarked 10-kilometre running trail.

RACE For more information or to register: *www.parkrun.org.uk/whinlatterforest*

WHAT NEXT? Other trail parkruns in England which are worth lacing up your shoes for include Tamar Trails, Dalby Forest, Lyme Park, Fell Foot, Black Park or The Pastures.

DISTANCE **5km** ASCENT **180m** TIME **0:20–0:40 hours**
RECORDS **19.56 minutes (F); 16.19 minutes (M)** START/FINISH
Whinlatter Forest Park main car park GRID REF **NY 208 244**
GPS **54.6085, -3.2277** PUBLIC TRANSPORT **Limited seasonal buses from Keswick (Stagecoach 77), but the timetable does not tie in well with the start of the weekly parkrun. It is possible to reach the park on foot from Thornthwaite village via a bridleway (2km)**
PARKING **Whinlatter Forest Park (parking charges apply)**
MORE INFO **www.forestryengland.uk/whinlatter**

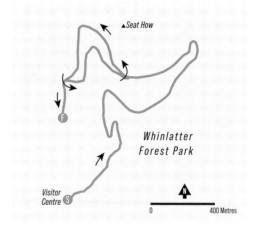

02
HAMPSTEAD HEATH

10km | **TRAIL** | **NAVIGATION** 2 partial waymarking
LONDON

Escape the city on this wonderful undulating loop of the historic Hampstead Heath, one of London's best-loved green spaces.

Hampstead Heath is an ancient London common which boasts an open-air lido (open all year), a butterfly house (Golders Hill Park area) and even a small zoo!

There are many interlinking trails across the Heath, connecting boating and fishing ponds, sports facilities and historical monuments.

This circular route starts at the cafe at Parliament Hill (a vantage point with a view over London which is protected by law) and tours the ponds, Hampstead Heath Extension and Golders Hill Park, as well as visiting the summit of Hampstead Heath, the highest natural point in London at 134 metres high, and the Kite Hill viewpoint.

A map of this route and two shorter trails is available through the City of London website, *www.cityoflondon.gov.uk*

OTHER OPTIONS If you want to go long, London is also home to the London Loop (a 242-kilometre circular trail) and Thames Path National Trail (298 kilometres from the source of the River Thames to Woolwich), which provide plentiful linear route options.

RACE There are many events that take place on the heath, including the Run for Your Life 10K, 5K and fun trail races organised by the Jubilee Hall Trust and Cancer Research UK's Race for Life Hampstead 10K.

WHAT NEXT? London has many parks which are popular with runners. Favourites include Greenwich Park, Queen Elizabeth Olympic Park, Primrose Hill, Hyde Park and Richmond Park. Perhaps you could run round them all? For information on the perimeter trails of London parks visit: *www.runnersguidetolondon.co.uk/london-park-perimeters.html*

© SHUTTERSTOCK/FELA SANU

DISTANCE **10km**   ASCENT **130m**   TIME **0:45-1:15 hours**
START/FINISH **Parliament Hill Cafe, Hampstead Heath**
GRID REF **TQ 282 861**   GPS **51.5592, -0.1520**   PUBLIC TRANSPORT
Accessible by bus, train (to Hampstead Heath or Gospel Oak) or by Tube then foot from Hampstead or Tufnell Park stations
PARKING **Not recommended**   MORE INFO **www.visitlondon.com/things-to-do/place/607535-hampstead-heath**

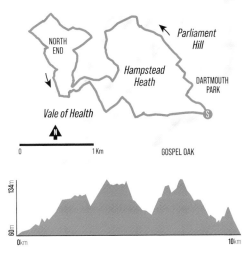

03

BROWN WILLY

9km | **TRAIL** | **NAVIGATION 3** no waymarking
CORNWALL

Run across a rugged moorland, littered with weather-sculpted granite tors, and tick off the highest summit in Cornwall.

DISTANCE **9km** ASCENT **260m** TIME **0:45–1:30 hours**
START/FINISH **Rough Tor car park** GRID REF **SX 138 819**
GPS **50.6070, -4.6328** PUBLIC TRANSPORT **None past Camelford
(4km by road to car park)** PARKING **Rough Tor car park (free)**
MORE INFO **www.bodminmoor.co.uk**

Bodmin Moor is quieter than its larger neighbour Dartmoor, but it is a similar landscape of legend and myth, where archaeological remains and wild ponies abound. An eerie mist can roll in quickly and unexpectedly here, so a map and compass are essential!

The route follows grassy trails initially which can be wet and boggy, heading round the bulk of Rough Tor. If you're lucky, you may spot the Rough Tor Holy Well (rediscovered and restored in 1994) before picking your way through the rocky ground.

From Little Rough Tor it's across a grassy col to the granite stack of Showery Tor, then the main trail leads down into the valley and towards Brown Willy (trig point at 420 metres). Nip along the summit ridge to visit the various Bronze Age cairns before doubling back to the bridge at the bottom of the valley and skirting back round the end of Rough Tor.

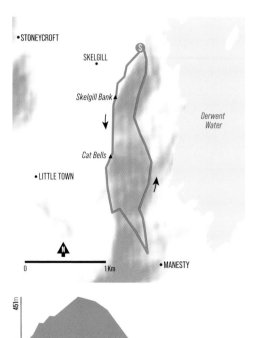

04

CAT BELLS

6km | **TRAIL** | **NAVIGATION 3** no waymarking
LAKE DISTRICT

A short classic of the Lake District. The climb up this distinctive and popular hill is richly rewarded with a stunning Lakeland panorama.

DISTANCE **6km** ASCENT **310m** TIME **1:00–1:40 hours**
START/FINISH **Hawse End, Derwent Water** GRID REF **NY 246 211**
GPS **54.5794, -3.1680** PUBLIC TRANSPORT **Accessible from Keswick
on foot (5km on roads and trails) or via the ferry to Hawse End**
PARKING **Small car parking area (often very busy) or park responsibly
on surrounding small roads. Do not park on double yellow lines or
blocking gates**

OTHER OPTIONS Brown Willy can also be reached from the south-east by starting in Bolventor. This 11-kilometre route takes in Tolborough and Catshole Tors on the way out, and returns via Priddacombe Downs and Roughlands Farm (missing out Rough Tor).

RACE The Brown Willy Run (purely a social run, not a race) is run by Truro Running Club. It takes place on New Year's Day, starting and finishing at the famous smugglers' haunt, the Jamaica Inn, *www.trurorunningclub.org.uk/trc-events/brown-willy-run*

WHAT NEXT? Other great moorland routes include trails around the Cheesewring and Caradon Hill (also Bodmin Moor). On Dartmoor, try a loop around Grimspound or a link-up of Widecombe in the Moor with Haytor and Hound Tor. If you are into ticking tors then take a look at the Ten Tors Challenge routes, organised by the British Army.

This accessible hill is situated close to the busy market town of Keswick and is one of the most popular routes in the Lakes.

Steep zigzags lead straight up the nose of the ridge, but it's worth pausing to enjoy the panoramic views of Derwent Water, which just keep getting better as you get higher. There are a couple of mild scrambly sections; these are easier than they look and can be tackled directly or by following small paths off to the side. Beyond the summit, it's all downhill, then back along the flank of Cat Bells to the start. Try to stick to the made path to avoid further erosion of the surrounding hillside.

OTHER OPTIONS To extend the route slightly, after the summit underneath Black Crag keep going on the bridleway and head into the woodland of Manesty Park. Follow the Cumbria Way north along the edge of Derwent Water past several bays to return to Hawse End.

For a longer challenge, try the Cat Bells, Maiden Moor and High Spy circular, or the classic Newlands Horseshoe, which takes in the six summits of Cat Bells, Maiden Moor, High Spy, Dale Head, Hindscarth, and Robinson. George Fisher's Tea Round (see page 38) takes in the summits, including Cat Bells, visible from the tea room at George Fisher in Keswick, as does its shorter sibling, the Espresso Round.

RACE There aren't any races on this specific route, but several longer races do take in this popular summit.

WHAT NEXT? For similar small hills in the Lake District try Silver How, Hay Stacks, Loughrigg Fell, Latrigg or Castlerigg Fell. Across Great Britain, try Roseberry Topping in North Yorkshire; Chrome Hill or Mam Tor in the Peak District; or Conic Hill next to Loch Lomond (see page 60).

05
PENDLE HILL

8km | **TRAIL** | **NAVIGATION 2** partial waymarking
LANCASHIRE

The classic circular of Pendle Hill is a short run on grassy trails. This modest hill has a strong fell racing pedigree.

DISTANCE **8km**   ASCENT **350m**   TIME **0:45–1:40 hours**
START/FINISH **Barley car park**   GRID REF **SD 823 403**
GPS **53.8586, -2.2705**   PUBLIC TRANSPORT **Nearest train stations are Colne, Nelson and Brierfield. The bus service between Clitheroe and Nelson calls at Barley**   PARKING **Barley car park (parking charges apply)**

Pendle Hill stands in the Forest of Bowland National Landscape and is renowned for its connection with the Pendle Witches and the 1612 Lancashire Witch Trials. The outbound section of this run (along the Pendle Way) is waymarked by a witch on her broomstick. The first fell race over the summit took place in 1956.

From Barley, the well-marked Pendle Way trail climbs steadily upwards, passing Ings End, Brown House and Pendle House to join the ridge path north of the trig point on Big End. The descent heads down Boar Clough into Ogden Clough, then along the valley past Upper and then Lower Ogden reservoirs.

OTHER OPTIONS For something much longer, the Pendle Way is a long-distance, circular trail that takes in Pendle Hill, starting and finishing in Barrowford (69 kilometres; 1,840 metres of ascent).

The three principal summits in the surrounding area (Pendle Hill, Weets Hill and Boulsworth Hill) can be linked together in what is known as Pendle's Three Peaks challenge.

RACE Pendle Hill is home to the short Pendle Fell Race, the Stan Bradshaw Pendle Round and the longer Tour of Pendle – arguably the classic of the three fell races, *www.wp.claytonlemoors.org.uk*, *www.tourofpendle.co.uk* The popular Pendle Way in a Day event covers the full 69 kilometres in winter and is open to both runners and walkers (shorter version also available), *www.pendlewayinaday.co.uk*

WHAT NEXT? Other small hills across the UK with a similar stature include Roseberry Topping, Worcestershire Beacon, Herefordshire Beacon, Chrome Hill, Castle Crag, Mynydd Carningli, Tryfan, Clachnaben, The Whangie, Box Hill, Brown Willy (see page 4), Mam Tor, Bow Hill or Stac Pollaidh, to name but a few!

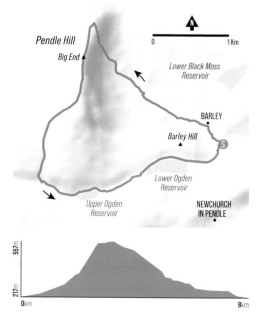

06

AVEBURY TO OGBOURNE ST GEORGE

15km | **TRAIL** | **NAVIGATION** 1 fully waymarked
WILTSHIRE

Follow the historically rich southern section of Britain's oldest road, The Ridgeway, a route used by travellers, herdsmen and soldiers since prehistoric times.

DISTANCE **15km** ASCENT **190m** TIME **1:45–2:15 hours**
START **The official start of The Ridgeway is Overton Hill but starting at the nearby village of Avebury gives better transport connections and more amenities** FINISH **Ogbourne St George** GRID REF **SU 099 696/ SU 199 744** GPS **51.4253, -1.8590/51.4682, -1.7149**
PUBLIC TRANSPORT **The start and finish are connected by bus (change at either Marlborough or Swindon)** PARKING **There are several car parks in Avebury village, as well as the Avebury National Trust car park (parking charges apply)**

The Ridgeway trail, taking the line of Britain's oldest road, is famed for the many archaeological monuments along its length, including Stone Age long barrows, Bronze Age round barrows, Iron Age forts and iconic figures of white horses cut into the chalky hillside.

Starting at the Avebury stone circle, a UNESCO World Heritage Site, the route follows The Ridgeway along high ground, crossing the road above the Hackpen White Horse, which is said to have been cut in 1838 to celebrate Queen Victoria's coronation. The trail also passes through the Barbury Castle hillfort, staying high as far as Upper Herdswick Farm, where it takes the line of Smeathe's Ridge, an airy traverse which offers spectacular views on both sides, with Liddington Castle to the north and the Marlborough Downs to the south.

Much of The Ridgeway is designated as a bridleway or byway, so you may meet horses, bicycles and even the odd motorbike!

OTHER OPTIONS Why not try other sections of The Ridgeway, such as the most remote section, Ogbourne St George to Sparsholt Firs (25 kilometres), the most strenuous section, Watlington to Wendover (27 kilometres), or the final wooded section from Wendover to Ivinghoe Beacon (19 kilometres), finishing in the beautiful Ashridge Estate.

The Ridgeway also forms part of the Greater Ridgeway, an even longer 597-kilometre challenge from the Dorset coast to the Norfolk coast!

RACE The iconic Race to the Stones 100-kilometre ultra takes place each July from Lewknor to Avebury, finishing at the Avebury stone circle. The event is organised by Threshold Sports and is part of the Threshold Trail Series.

WHAT NEXT? For more challenges with an archaeological flavour, consider sections of Hadrian's Wall Path, St Cuthbert's Way or the Cotswold Way terminating in the Roman city of Bath. The 180-kilometre Icknield Way Path is also part of the Greater Ridgeway route.

© SHUTTERSTOCK/LANAG

07

WESTHUMBLE TO MERSTHAM

17km | **TRAIL** | **NAVIGATION** 1 fully waymarked
SURREY

An urban escape in the Surrey Hills on this challenging short section of the North Downs Way, taking in the popular viewpoint of Box Hill.

From Westhumble cross the River Mole on attractive stepping stones (after heavy rain you will need to use the bridge) then ascend Box Hill on the well-signposted North Downs Way. There is a National Trust visitor centre at the top with breathtaking views across the North Downs. From here the trail sweeps down through woodland, followed by a second fairly steep climb back up towards the Brockham Hills. The trail undulates along to Reigate Hill, where there are the remains of a small Victorian fort, then continues into National Trust woodland, and through Gatton Park.

OTHER OPTIONS There are several circular routes around Box Hill – these can be found at *www.nationaltrust.org. uk/box-hill*

ULTRA ROUTE This challenge is part of the North Downs Way National Trail, which is easily accessible from London and offers 246 kilometres of undulating trail. It links two National Landscapes – the Surrey Hills and the Kent Downs – and takes the path of the famous Pilgrims' Way from Winchester to Canterbury. The FKT is held by (M) Leroy Valentine with 1:19:33.00 in 2024.

DISTANCE **17km**   ASCENT **360m**   TIME **1:45–2:30 hours**
START **Box Hill & Westhumble railway station**
FINISH **Merstham railway station**   GRID REF **TQ 167 518/TQ 291 532**
GPS **51.2537, -0.3287/51.2633, -0.1510**   PUBLIC TRANSPORT **The start and finish can be linked by train or bus (not direct)**   PARKING **Car parks at both stations – Box Hill & Westhumble (free) and Merstham (parking charges apply)**

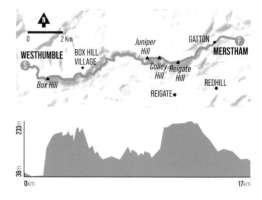

RACE The North Downs Way 50 and 100 events are organised by Centurion Running. There is also the North Downs Ridge 50k (from Freedom Racing) and the North Downs Way Ultra Run (from Running Adventures).

WHAT NEXT? If you enjoyed this challenge, consider other sections of this National Trail or the nearby South Downs Way, which covers the entire length of the South Downs National Park from Winchester to Eastbourne. This more southerly alternative is also easily accessible from London.

08
HELVELLYN EDGES

14km | FELL | NAVIGATION 3 *no waymarking*
LAKE DISTRICT

The ultimate way to climb England's third highest mountain – scramble up one narrow, iconic ridge and down another.

DISTANCE **14km** ASCENT **820m** TIME **2-3 hours** START/FINISH
Glenridding GRID REF **NY 386 169** GPS **54.5437, -2.9491**
PUBLIC TRANSPORT **Glenridding has good bus connections with nearby towns** PARKING **Glenridding car park (parking charges apply)**

© JOHN COEFIELD

Helvellyn is said to be the most popular mountain in the Lake District, and much of this popularity is due to the striking ridges on its craggy eastern side. Two of these, Striding Edge and Swirral Edge, top out on either side of the summit trig.

The route heads out of Glenridding village, passing the Travellers Rest pub, and up to the Hole-in-the-Wall at the foot of Striding Edge. This is a grade 1 scramble with considerable exposure in places and is often very busy. There are easier and harder options along its length, so choose your route carefully. At the top, there is a memorial to artist Charles Gough and his faithful dog. The summit plateau is very flat (in 1926 an aeroplane successfully landed and took off again). There are fantastic 360-degree views, and it is said that on a clear day you can see Blackpool Tower.

Descent is via Swirral Edge (also a grade 1 scramble). This is often much quieter than Striding Edge and is also a bit easier, but there is still plenty of exposure. The ridge leads to the summit of Catstye Cam before a pleasant descent into Keppel Cove and back to Glenridding.

OTHER OPTIONS An easier way to climb Helvellyn is as an out-and-back route from Wythburn at the southern end of Thirlmere. To extend the adventure, miss out Swirral Edge and follow the plateau south over Nethermost Pike, High Crag and Dollywaggon Pike.

Go on to Patterdale and Glenridding either via the Grisedale Valley or over St Sunday Crag (with an optional grade 3 scramble on Pinnacle Ridge).

RACE The Pinnacle Ridge Extreme skyrace takes in much of this route, including both of the Helvellyn edges, *www.lakedistrictskytrails.com* There is also the less technical Grisedale Horseshoe Fell Race, starting and finishing in Glenridding, *www.achille-ratti-climbing-club.co.uk*

WHAT NEXT? Other top scrambles in the Lake District that can be incorporated into great mountain running days include Sharp Edge on Blencathra, Cam Crag Ridge on Glaramara or Jack's Rake on Pavey Ark. Elsewhere in Great Britain try the Ben Nevis Horseshoe or Tryfan and Bristly Ridge in Eryri; the Fiacaill Ridge in the Cairngorms; or the longer Ring of Steall in the Western Highlands (see page 82). For something harder, try the Aonach Eagach traverse in Glen Coe or the Liathach traverse in Wester Ross.

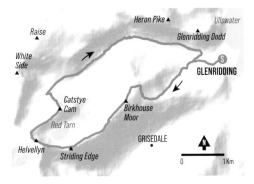

09
ISLE OF PORTLAND

20km | TRAIL | NAVIGATION 1 fully waymarked
DORSET

A clifftop loop around this limestone island
which marks the southernmost tip of the
stunning Jurassic Coast, a World Heritage Site.

| DISTANCE **20km** ASCENT **300m** TIME **2-3 hours**
| START/FINISH **Portland Harbour** GRID REF **SY 669 754**
| GPS **50.5780, -2.4686** PUBLIC TRANSPORT **The island is accessible**
| **by bus from Weymouth, which also has train connections**
| PARKING **Chesil car park, Portland (parking charges apply)**

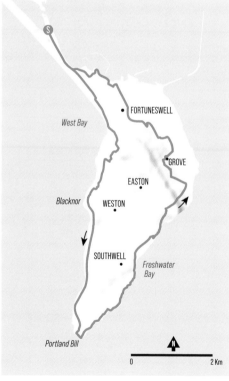

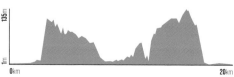

The tied island of Portland is connected to the
mainland by Chesil Beach – a 29-kilometre strip of
shingle which is one of the most iconic landmarks in
Dorset. The Portland Coast Path is an extension of
the waymarked South West Coast Path, so is easy to
follow. This route can be tackled in either direction,
but heading anticlockwise means that you finish
along the less industrial eastern side of the island.

This route offers unfailing views of the English
Channel and passes some fascinating sights as it
undulates along the cliffs, including an Olympic
Rings sculpture as well as coastal fortifications from
throughout the island's history – 19th-century Verne
Citadel, 20th-century Blacknor Fort, and 15th-century
Rufus Castle. At the southern tip of the island stands
the distinctive Portland Bill Lighthouse; you can climb
the 153 steps for panoramic views at top. You can also
visit Church Ope Cove, a sheltered beach that was once
sandy but is now covered with rounded pebbles. Just
don't mention the long-eared furry things – mentioning
the word 'rabbit' is frowned upon on the island!

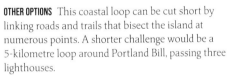

OTHER OPTIONS This coastal loop can be cut short by linking roads and trails that bisect the island at numerous points. A shorter challenge would be a 5-kilometre loop around Portland Bill, passing three lighthouses.

RACE The island is home to the Portland Coastal marathon, half marathon and 10K (from BustinSkin Events) and the Jurassic Extinction Ultra event from Climb South West, which includes a full loop of Portland.

WHAT NEXT? Other memorable areas of the Jurassic Coast include sections of the South West Coast Path around Lulworth Cove, Durdle Door, the sea stacks of Ladram Bay and Old Harry Rocks. Other impressive coastal routes can be found around Hartland in Devon; Tintagel in Cornwall; Beachy Head and the Seven Sisters (see page 17); the Castlemartin Peninsula in Pembrokeshire; and sections of the Isle of Anglesey Coastal Path including around Bwa Gwyn.

10

NINE STANDARDS RIGG

19km | **FELL** | **NAVIGATION** **4** difficult self-navigation or complex terrain
CUMBRIA

A run across Pennine moorland near Kirkby Stephen to visit the intriguing hilltop cairns of Nine Standards Rigg, taking in part of Wainwright's Coast to Coast trail.

DISTANCE **19km**	ASCENT **540m**	TIME **2:30-3:30 hours**

START/FINISH **Kirkby Stephen** GRID REF **NY 774 088**
GPS **54.4744, -2.3490** PUBLIC TRANSPORT **Kirkby Stephen has bus and rail links with surrounding towns** PARKING **Christian Head car park (free)**

Summarised by fell runner Carl Bell as 'A long pull up, then a long descent back', this route is worth it for the views. The best are to be seen from the Nine Standards, rather than from the summit trig point, with Cross Fell visible to the north-west and the Howgills to the south-west, as well as the High Street range of the eastern Lake District. The Nine Standards are a group of cairns, some of which were originally more than four metres high, which top Nine Standards Rigg, the summit of Hartley Fell. Their purpose is uncertain, but it is possible that they once marked the boundary between Westmorland and Swaledale.

GOOD TO KNOW Due to the bogginess of the terrain and the risk of erosion on Nine Standards Rigg, there are three different route variations recommended for different seasons over this part of Wainwright's Coast to Coast trail. Trail users are advised to avoid the path from the upper part of Faraday Gill to Nine Standards Rigg from December to April – take the path south above Dunderdale instead. Route variations are signposted and more information is available at *www.skyware.co.uk/c2c/maps.htm*

OTHER OPTIONS To explore more of Wainwright's Coast to Coast trail, consider running the section from Kirkby Stephen to Keld, an 18-kilometre through-route across open (and in places boggy) moorland with enchanting views to the Yorkshire Dales. Alternatively, run from Shap to Kirkby Stephen, which is considerably longer but drier and less challenging in terms of navigation.

ULTRA ROUTE Nine Standards Rigg is a memorable landmark and a significant obstacle on Wainwright's Coast to Coast trail, a network of trails linked together by the great Alfred Wainwright which begins at St Bees and concludes at Robin Hood's Bay. The 292-kilometre trail passes through three national parks – the Lake District, the Yorkshire Dales and the North

York Moors. The FKTs belong to (F) Sarah Perry in 2:07:26.04 in 2021 and (M) Damian Hall 1:15:18.40 in 2021, breaking Mike Hartley's record which had stood for almost 30 years.

RACE The 13-kilometre Nine Standards race takes place on New Year's Day. There is also a self-supported ultra from Ourea Events along Wainwright's Coast to Coast trail called the Northern Traverse, *www.northerntraverse.com*

WHAT NEXT? Other great places to run in the surrounding area include the Yorkshire Three Peaks (see page 35); Cosh; Malham Cove; Cautley Spout and The Calf; Maiden Castle; Keld and the Tan Hill Inn; and various sections of the Pennine Way.

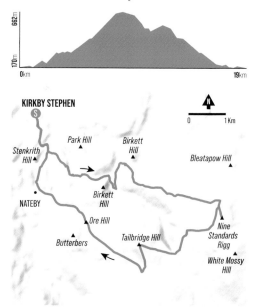

11
MALVERN HILLS

20km | **TRAIL** | **NAVIGATION** 2 partial waymarking
HEREFORDSHIRE AND WORCESTERSHIRE

Run the full ridgeline of the Malvern Hills which rise dramatically above the Severn Plain on the border of Herefordshire and Worcestershire.

DISTANCE **20km**   ASCENT **590m**   TIME **2:30–3:30 hours**
START **Malvern Link railway station**   FINISH **Ledbury railway station**
GRID REF **SO 782 474/SO 709 386**   GPS **52.1251, -2.3194/52.0452, -2.4253**   PUBLIC TRANSPORT **Regular, direct trains run between Malvern and Ledbury**   PARKING **Car parks at both stations (parking charges apply)**

© WILLIAM HOLYOAK

The Malvern Hills are a designated National Landscape and a Site of Special Scientific Interest. This route passes two large Iron Age hillforts – Midsummer Hill and British Camp.

Although the Malverns are only 425 metres at their highest point, the surrounding landscape is relatively flat, giving them an unexpected prominence and offering spectacular views as far as the Bristol Channel. Once up on the hills, the route is constantly undulating, taking in the northern section of the Malvern Hills, with the start and finish easily linked via train. Each hill has its charms, but Pinnacle Hill is particularly popular with paragliders.

OTHER OPTIONS   There are loads of trails in the hills and some handy car parks at the base of the hills if you're driving – trails around Worcestershire Beacon and British Camp are a good bet.

RACE   The Malvern Hills Trail Half Marathon links low-level trails to the west of the Malverns with some of the northern summits in a runnable circular route; for more information or to enter, visit *www.davetalbot.net*

WHAT NEXT?   The Bath Skyline is a 10-kilometre waymarked route across varied terrain (including some road) through the green spaces around the city of Bath, a World Heritage Site. The Frome Valley Trail in Dorset and the northerly sections of the Cotswold Way are other good options. Trails in the Wye Valley and the Brecon Beacons National Park just over the Welsh border offer limitless trail running opportunities.

12

BEACHY HEAD AND THE SEVEN SISTERS

24km | **TRAIL** | **NAVIGATION 2** partial waymarking
EAST SUSSEX

Grassy running along iconic white sea cliffs on a section of the South Downs Way to reach the highest chalk cliff in Britain.

© SHUTTERSTOCK/NICK HAWKES

DISTANCE **24km**   ASCENT **450m**   TIME **2:45–3:45 hours**
START/FINISH **Beachy Head**   GRID REF **TV 590 959**   GPS **50.7415, 0.2533**
PUBLIC TRANSPORT **The 13X bus runs between Eastbourne and Brighton (Sundays only), stopping at Beachy Head. For better transport links, extend the route slightly by starting in the centre of Eastbourne**
PARKING **Beachy Head car park (parking charges apply)**

The famous chalk Seven Sisters cliffs are the jaw-dropping highlight of one of the longest stretches of undeveloped coastline on the South Coast, between Seaford and Eastbourne. But stay well back – the crumbling edges are unstable and undercut in places.

From Beachy Head, the route follows the South Downs Way skirting around the edge of Eastbourne and up Willingdon Hill, then heads through Friston Forest to Westdean, meeting the coastline near Cliff End. Undulating grassy running leads back east over the hills of the Seven Sisters. Each of the seven chalk cliffs has a name, and an eighth sibling is being eroded by the relentless battering of the sea. Waymarkers lead past Birling Gap to Beachy Head, the highest chalk cliff in Britain at 162 metres high, with its iconic lighthouse below.

OTHER OPTIONS This route can be shortened by running only the coastline section (Westdean to Beachy Head) as a linear route. Alternatively, the run can be lengthened by following the route of the famous Beachy Head Marathon – or the ultra (see right).

ULTRA ROUTE The South Downs Way is a 160-kilometre trail which follows old droveways along the chalk escarpment and ridges of the South Downs, from Winchester to Eastbourne. Centurion Running's South Downs Way 100 takes in the full length of the South Downs Way; course records are (F) Bethan Male at 16:49.57 in 2022 and (M) Mark Perkins with 14:03.54 in 2014.

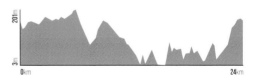

RACE The Beachy Head Ultramarathon (53 kilometres), Marathon, Half Marathon and 10K all take place in October, *www.visiteastbourne.com/marathon*

WHAT NEXT? What next? For a similar experience, try running over the White Cliffs of Dover (from Dover to Deal), which is part of the England Coast Path. Other dramatic coastal challenges in Great Britain include the Isle of Portland (see page 12); sections of the South West Coast Path (such as St Ives to Penzance, or along the Jurassic Coast); the Hebridean Way; the Fife Coastal Path; the Moray Coast Trail; and sections of the Pembrokeshire Coast Path.

13
COLEDALE HORSESHOE

15km | **FELL** | **NAVIGATION** 3 no waymarking
LAKE DISTRICT

A traditional fell-running circuit over runnable grassy hills and superb ridgelines, linking the five Wainwright fells surrounding the Coledale Valley.

DISTANCE **15km** ASCENT **970m** TIME **2:15–3:15 hours**
START/FINISH **Braithwaite** GRID REF **NY 229 236** GPS **54.6017, -3.1945**
PUBLIC TRANSPORT **Regular buses run along the A66** PARKING **Some on-street parking in Braithwaite – please park considerately**

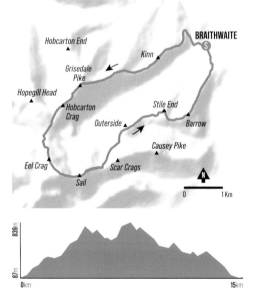

This challenge is one of the great Lakeland horseshoes, and is often quieter than the others. This fabulous middle-distance fell-running route also has plenty of options for variation.

Starting from Braithwaite, the round takes in Grisedale Pike; Eel Crag (usually known as Crag Hill) at the centre of the horseshoe and its highpoint; Sail, with its iconic zigzags down the far side; heather-covered Outerside; and Barrow. There are a few scrambly sections and some glorious Lakeland ridgeline, encircling the spectacular hanging valley of Coledale.

OTHER OPTIONS This challenge is just one version of the Coledale Horseshoe. If you have extra energy, extend the route by including Hopegill Head. If you're a glutton-for-punishment, include Grasmoor, Wandope, Scar Crags and Causey Pike too.

RACE The popular Coledale Horseshoe fell race takes place annually in spring and is a classic of the race calendar; it is organised by Ellenborough Athletic Club. The course records are held by (F) V. Wilkinson at 01:17.38 in 2017 and (M) J. Symonds at 01:07.45 in 2012.

WHAT NEXT? Other great Lakeland rounds include the Ennerdale Horseshoe, the Fairfield Horseshoe, the Newlands Round, the Mickleden Round, the Kentmere Horseshoe and the Deepdale Horseshoe. In Wales try the Yr Wyddfa/Snowdon Horseshoe in Eryri (see page 136); the Waun Fach Horseshoe in the Black Mountains; or the Brecon Beacons Horseshoe. In Scotland good options include the Ballachulish Horsehoe or the Glenfinnan Munros in the Western Highlands; the Glen Lyon Horseshoe in Perth and Kinross; or the runnable Munros of Glen Feshie in the Cairngorms.

14

SHERINGHAM TO SEA PALLING

37km | TRAIL | NAVIGATION 1 fully waymarked
NORFOLK

Run along the shore and clifftops on this stunning section of the Norfolk Coast Path, finishing with a dip at a beautiful sandy beach!

DISTANCE **37km** ASCENT **240m** TIME **3:30–4:30 hours**
START **Sheringham** FINISH **Sea Palling** GRID REF **TG 159 434/TG 429 274**
GPS **52.9451, 1.2126/52.7897, 1.6024** PUBLIC TRANSPORT **The Coasthopper bus service travels along the north Norfolk coast linking King's Lynn and Mundesley. There is also a bus service linking Sea Palling to this network via North Walsham** PARKING **Various options in Sheringham and Sea Palling**

Hug the coastline through a National Landscape on this scenic stretch of the Norfolk Coast Path. The trail sticks to the coast with only a couple of minor diversions inland. At Mundesley and Sea Palling, you can run along the beach if you wish.

The waymarked trail begins by heading up to the Beeston Bump viewpoint, used as a secret listening station during World War II. The bump is part of the Cromer Ridge, created during glacier retreat at the end of the last ice age.

There are many Sites of Special Scientific Interest to enjoy along the way, including the West Runton Cliffs, where the enormous West Runton mammoth skeleton was discovered in 1990.

The route also visits Cromer with its seawall and promenade, Overstrand – the 'Village of Millionaires' – and Happisburgh, with its iconic red-and-white-banded lighthouse. After passing through the Marram Hills, a shoreline county wildlife site, you finish at the calm waters of Sea Palling beach.

OTHER OPTIONS A shorter and simpler version of this challenge would be to run the 7 kilometres between the towns of Sheringham and Cromer, which are connected by a rail link. To extend the challenge, just keep running! Your day can be terminated at any of the coastal villages and towns along the route (many are connected by bus).

ULTRA ROUTE The Norfolk Coast Path is a 135-kilometre waymarked trail from Hunstanton to Hopton-on-Sea. The FKT belongs to (F) Fiona Manders at 19:15.51 in 2021 and (M) Jack Mollicone at 13:28.09 in 2020. In combination with the adjoining Peddars Way, it is a recognised National Trail.

RACE There are several trail races along the Norfolk Coast Path including the Norfolk Coastal Trail Marathon and Half Marathon (from Positive Steps).

WHAT NEXT? For other long-distance coastal trails, take a look at the Cleveland Way between Saltburn-by-the-Sea and Scarborough; the Moray Coast Trail; the Fife Coastal Path; the Pembrokeshire Coast Path; or the enormous South West Coast Path.

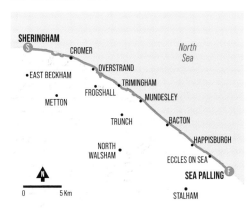

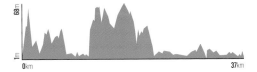

15

MIDDLETON-IN-TEESDALE TO DUFTON

33km | **FELL** | **NAVIGATION** 1 fully waymarked
NORTH PENNINES

Pass through meadows, along rocky ravines and past thundering waterfalls on this stunning section of the Pennine Way to reach the enormous U-shaped valley and spellbinding scenery at High Cup Nick.

Snaking up the mountainous spine of the UK, the Pennine Way is Britain's first and best known National Trail. This route runs along one of its most dramatic sections, with sights such as the wobbly Wynch Bridge (opened in around 1830 and with capacity for only one person at a time), Keith Alexander's stone Sheep sculpture, the Low Force waterfall and its big sibling High Force, a real highlight at 21 metres in height and one of the most impressive waterfalls in England. The buildings around Forest-in-Teesdale are all painted white, reputedly at the insistence of a landowner in the valley who wished to always be able to identify his own properties. It is possible to make a short detour to the Langdon Beck Hotel for lunch if you wish, before you leave the valley and climb up on to the moors.

The limestone Falcon Clints which border Widdybank Fell block out the view and roar of Cauldron Snout until you are almost upon it. These falls can be very impressive after heavy rain and the rocky path up the side of the waterfall is quite an experience! The final highlight of the route is High Cup Nick; looking out over High Cup Gill, a huge U-shaped valley carved out of the hillside, you can enjoy the most memorable viewpoint on the Pennine Way before dropping down into Dufton to finish.

OTHER OPTIONS A shorter (16-kilometre) circular option starts at Hanging Shaw car park in Teesdale and joins the Pennine Way at Cronkley Bridge, taking the short scramble up the side of Cauldron Snout to gain a trail heading north past the Cow Green Reservoir dam. Return to Teesdale along the access road.

The initial river section from Middleton-in-Teesdale can be extended with a 4-kilometre stretch of the Teesdale Way starting at Egglesburn.

DISTANCE **33km** ASCENT **500m** TIME **3:30–4:30 hours**
START **Middleton-in-Teesdale** FINISH **Dufton** GRID REF **NY 946 255/NY 689 250** GPS **54.6250, -2.0836/54.6195, -2.4825**
PUBLIC TRANSPORT **No practical options** PARKING **One car park and limited on-street parking in Middleton-in-Teesdale; free parking available in Dufton**

ULTRA ROUTE Arguably Great Britain's most famous National Trail, the full Pennine Way is a 431-kilometre trail along the length of the Pennines from Edale in the Peak District to Kirk Yetholm in the Scottish Borders. The FKTs belong to (F) Anna Troup at 3:00:46.37 in 2021 and (M) John Kelly at 2:10:04.53 in 2021.

RACE The infamous Montane Spine Race runs the full length of the Pennine Way; there are winter and summer versions. There are also three shorter options in both seasons: the Sprint, the Challenger and the Challenger North. Short but sharp, the Cronkley Fell Race starts in Holwick, crosses Cronkley Fell and descends to the River Tees, before returning via the same route (17 kilometres with around 560 metres of ascent).

WHAT NEXT? Similar scale challenges to the full Pennine Way include the Offa's Dyke Path or the South West Coast Path. For remote and hilly trails consider the Southern Upland Way, the Dales High Way or the Cleveland Way.

Great Dun Fell

Cow Green
Reservoir

0   3 Km

Meldon Hill

Haugh Hill

Hare Hill

Rasp Hill

Green Hill

KNOCK

Dufton
Pike

High Cup
Nick

Noon Hill

MIDDLETON-IN-
TEESDALE

DUFTON

S

Peeping Hill

Murton Fell

Mickle Fell

BRAMPTON

Murton Pike

Standards

16

CHOLLERFORD TO GREENHEAD

31km | **TRAIL** | **NAVIGATION** **1** fully waymarked
NORTHUMBERLAND

Traverse the most dramatic and best-preserved section of historic Hadrian's Wall, a World Heritage Site which once marked the northern boundary of the Roman Empire.

DISTANCE **31km**   ASCENT **560m**   TIME **3:30–4:15 hours**
START **Chollerford**   FINISH **Greenhead**   GRID REF **NY 919 706/NY 659 653**
GPS **55.0298, -2.1280/54.9819, -2.5343**   PUBLIC TRANSPORT **The Hadrian's Wall Bus (AD122) runs regularly between Hexham and Walltown, stopping at Greenhead and Chollerford**   PARKING **On-street parking in Chollerford; Thirlwall View car park (free) near Greenhead**

Hadrian's Wall is one of the most famous historical landmarks in Britain; Hadrian's Wall Path – the only waymarked coast-to-coast trail across England – runs along its length. This bite-sized challenge begins at the the 18th-century five-arch bridge at Chollerford, then follows the waymarked trail west past numerous Roman sights – Brocolitia Temple, Coventina's Well, the Temple of Mithras and Housesteads Fort (close to Vindolanda, where some fascinating examples of writing tablets were discovered).

Around halfway through this challenge, Hadrian's Wall Path crosses the Pennine Way at Cuddy's Crags. The running is extremely pleasant here, and you can work up a thirst over the undulating countryside and link a number of craggy escarpments before heading into the village of Once Brewed for a pint of the famous Twice Brewed Bitter!

Back on the trail, there's a gradual climb up to the highest viewpoint on the wall, Green Slack on Winshield Crags, where there are superb views in every direction. The way heads on over Walltown Crags and down towards the village of Greenhead and the ruins of the 12th-century Thirlwall Castle (strengthened with stone repurposed from the Wall).

OTHER OPTIONS   The sections of Hadrian's Wall Path to the east and west of this one have a different character and are less taxing overall, especially as they approach the coast. For the full challenge, why not complete the entire trail over two or three days, *www.hadrianswallcountry.co.uk*

ULTRA ROUTE   The Hadrian's Wall Path is a 135-kilometre National Trail stretching coast to coast across Northern England, from Wallsend in the east to Bowness-on-Solway on the west coast. It follows the line of the Hadrian's Wall UNESCO World Heritage Site and is littered with historical sites and museums. The FKT for the full distance belongs to (F) Izzy Millburn at 18:42.51 in 2018 and (M) Ellis Bland at 13:18.43 in 2021.

WHAT NEXT?   For other long-distance trails with a historical feel, try sections of the John Muir Way, Cotswold Way, The Ridgeway, Great Glen Way or the super-long Offa's Dyke Path.

N

0   3 Km

BARRASFORD

Limestone
Bank

HUMSHAUGH

Haughton
Common

Greenlee
Lough

Sewingshields
Crags

S
CHOLLERFORD

Crag Lough

Clew Hill   Howden Hill

WALL

FOURSTONES

NEWBROUGH

Winshield Crags

ACOMB

BARDON MILL

GREENHEAD   HALTWHISTLE   HAYDON BRIDGE

HEXHAM

MELKRIDGE   REDBURN

17

EDALE SKYLINE

33km | FELL | NAVIGATION 4 difficult self-navigation
or complex terrain
PEAK DISTRICT

The ultimate high-level circular in the Peak
District, linking the ridges and hills of the
Vale of Edale.

> DISTANCE **33km** ASCENT **830m** TIME **4:30-5:30 hours** START/FINISH
> **Hope railway station** GRID REF **SK 180 832** GPS **53.3460, -1.7296**
> PUBLIC TRANSPORT **Regular trains between Sheffield and Manchester
> Piccadilly stop at Hope** PARKING **Hope car park (parking charges apply)**

The Edale Skyline is the Peak District's best-known fell
running challenge and is associated with a classic but
testing race that dates back to 1974. It is an aesthetic
and runnable round, skirting the Kinder Plateau and
crossing remote high moorland, with beautiful views
over the Vale of Edale.

The route is packed with interest. Starting in the
picturesque village of Hope, climb up Win Hill for
some panoramic views, then head along an old Roman
Road, passing the Hope Cross – this is actually a tall
square pillar whose capstone bears the names of Hope,
Sheffield, Glossop and Edale. Contour the Kinder
plateau via the rocks at Ringing Roger and the gritstone
outcrop of Upper Tor. Just beyond the halfway point at
Crowden Tower are the Wool Packs, naturally sculpted
gritstone boulders that resemble animals and faces in
the mist. Take care not to get stuck in the peat bog!

More solid paving slabs lead over Brown Knoll,
and after a remote section you reach the spectacular
ridgeline of Lord's Seat. It just keeps getting better as
you follow the Great Ridge from Mam Tor to Lose
Hill – the paved ridge is the finest in the Peak District –
before descending back to Hope.

OTHER OPTIONS Extend the route by starting at Edale
(which also has a railway station) or by adding in an
out-and-back to Kinder Scout. Shorten by descending
to Edale at Grindsbrook Clough or Crowden Clough,
then climb up and over Hollins Cross to return to
Hope (or catch the train for one stop). For cosy
character and good food, pop into The Old Nag's Head
in Edale, which marks the start of the Pennine Way.

© JAMIE RUTHERFORD

RACE The Don Morrison Memorial Edale Skyline
fell race starts and finishes at Edale. The course has
changed over the years due to restrictions and trail
maintenance – it is organised by the Dark Peak Fell
Runners. The Kinder Downfall fell race is organised by
Pennine Fell Runners.

WHAT NEXT? This challenge is useful preparation for the
Yorkshire Three Peaks (see page 35). Alternatively,
try other sections of the Pennine Way or the Nine
Edges of the Peak District (see page 28). Other
options across Great Britain include the Kentmere and
Ennerdale skylines in the Lake District or the Pentland
Skyline in Southern Scotland (see page 94). For an
ultra-distance challenge in the Peak District, try the
Derwent Watershed (see page 36).

© JAMIE RUTHERFORD

© JAMIE RUTHERFORD

Ladybower
Reservoir
Crookstone
Knoll
Kinder
Scout
Upper Tor
Kinder
Low
Wooler
Knoll
Grindslow Knoll
NETHER BOOTH
UPPER BOOTH
EDALE
Lose
Hill
Win Hill
Brown
Knoll
BARBER BOOTH
Mam Tor
HOPE
ASTON
Lord's
Seat
CASTLETON
BROUGH
BRADWELL
0   2 Km

625m

161m

0km   33km

© JON BARTON

18
HOWGILL FELLS

21km | FELL | NAVIGATION 4 difficult self-navigation or complex terrain
YORKSHIRE DALES

A quintessentially tough fell running challenge through the rugged but beautiful Howgill Fells – expect pathless, thigh-bursting climbs and tussocks aplenty.

DISTANCE **21km**   ASCENT **1,900m**   TIME **5–6 hours**
START/FINISH **Sedbergh**   GRID REF **SD 655 922**   GPS **54.3242, -2.5319**
PUBLIC TRANSPORT **Irregular bus services to surrounding towns**
PARKING **Various options in Sedbergh (parking charges apply)**

The Howgills are a small range of rounded grassy hills that are often overlooked on account of their proximity to the neighbouring Lake District and the better-known parts of the Yorkshire Dales, but in fact the area has a quiet, rough beauty all of its own and some excellent fell running.

At first glance, this route appears to be a pleasant jaunt to the tops of the more interesting hills near Sedbergh, including the popular fell of The Calf, which is the highest point in the Howgills. This is a roller coaster of a route, with six main leg-shredding climbs and more than a few extra ones which you'll certainly consider to be climbs when you're doing them. To be honest, most of it feels like it's straight up or straight

down and fording the becks feels like the only bit of brief respite.

Luckily from Winder, the final summit on the route, you head straight down towards Lockbank Farm (famous for its delicious home-made ice cream, including local favourite flavour, Howgill Hurricane), and from there it's a short sprint to the finish to rest your trembling quads.

OTHER OPTIONS For a taster, try climbing Crook, then cut directly across to Arant Haw and back to Sedbergh. The Howgills Trail 13 (Montane Trail Series) is only slightly shorter than this route but has around half the amount of ascent. For a linear journey, follow the Dales High Way National Trail from Sedbergh to Bowderdale.

RACE This route follows the course of the Howgills Fell Race, which last took place in 2018. The Sedbergh Hills Fell Race (24 kilometres with 1,350 metres of ascent) is another local classic – it is a little more 'runnable' than the Howgills Fell Race.

WHAT NEXT? For other rough fell running challenges like this, try the Paps of Jura (see page 78), the shorter Ras y Moelwyn or the longer Fellsman (see page 48). If you like an element of surprise, enter the OMM – Original Mountain Marathon – for a similar experience over two days. For the ultimate multi-day rough running challenge, try the Dragon's Back Race or the Meirionnydd Round (see page 124).

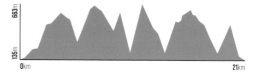

© STEPHEN WILSON www.grandadayoutphotography.co.uk

19
NINE EDGES

36km | **FELL** | **NAVIGATION 3** no waymarking
PEAK DISTRICT

Link nine gritstone edges in one of the UK's
most loved national parks.

DISTANCE **36km** ASCENT **750m** TIME **5–6 hours**
RECORDS **(F) S. Fawcett 2:48:00 in 2013; (M) D. Palmer 2:26:00 in 2013**
START **Fairholmes, Ladybower Reservoir** FINISH **Robin Hood pub, Baslow**
GRID REF **SK 172 893/SK 280 721** GPS **53.4002, -1.7427/53.2451, -1.5818**
PUBLIC TRANSPORT **No practical options** PARKING **Fairholmes car
park at the start and Birchen Edge car park at the end (parking
charges apply)**

The striking gritstone escarpments of the Peak District
are unique geological features that jut out of the
heathery landscape. These edges are a mecca for rock
climbers from all over the world, and many famous
climbers have cut their teeth on these short technical
walls. This running challenge links the finest gritstone
edges in a linear route that spans the OS Explorer Dark
Peak and White Peak maps and passes three cosy inns
along the way.

From Ladybower, you tackle the two longest edges
first, ticking off Derwent and Stanage. These are
followed by Burbage North and South (yes, these are
definitely two separate edges), then Froggatt Edge
which is neatly linked to Curbar and Baslow. The route
heads through beautiful woodland to the final two
edges, Gardom's and Birchen. At the top of Birchen
Edge, you'll find Nelson's Monument (erected long
before the column in London) and nearby, the 'Ship
Rocks' – outcrops carved with the names of three of
Nelson's ships, *Victory, Defiance* and *Royal Soverin* (sic).
From here, head down Birchen Edge to finish at the
Robin Hood Inn.

Most of the route is easy going, with no sharp ridges
or massive ascents, so this an ideal way to dip your toes
into longer distance challenges.

OTHER OPTIONS There are numerous variations on this
challenge and routes linking fewer gritstone edges.
If you prefer running shorter routes, you could collect
the nine edges over multiple trips. But if you only
choose one edge to run, the most striking and popular
is Stanage Edge.

RACE Edale Mountain Rescue Team organises the Nine
Edges event each year, which provides checkpoints,
support and a bus back to the start. It is open to
runners, walkers and rock climbers, *www.edalemrt.co.uk/
nine-edges*

WHAT NEXT? Alternative challenges in the Peak District
include the Derwent Watershed (see page 36),
Dovedale Dipper and the Edale Skyline (see page
24). If you're up for an epic challenge, the SkyNine
Challenge links up the Edale Skyline and the Nine
Edges. If you love quirky geological features, check out
Beachy Head and the Seven Sisters (see page 17); the
tors of Dartmoor in Devon; the spooky Quiraing on
the Isle of Skye; or the High Cup Nick (see page 20) or
Malham Cove sections of the Pennine Way.

20
CHEVY CHASE

31km | FELL | NAVIGATION 4 difficult self-navigation or complex terrain
NORTHUMBERLAND

© SHUTTERSTOCK/JOHN LOWINGS

A circular journey through the 'land of the far horizon' to summit The Cheviot, the highest point in Northumberland National Park.

The rolling hills of the Cheviots straddle the border of England and Scotland. Their highest point, The Cheviot, is an extinct volcano and is the last major peak on the Pennine Way. The popular Chevy Chase event has been taking place around midsummer for over 60 years. Initially a hiking challenge, it now welcomes both hikers and runners and is always oversubscribed.

From Wooler, the route follows trails south-west, passing between Broadhope Hill and Blackseat Hill before climbing steeply up to Scald Hill and eventually, after a few false summits, a ladder stile and paving slabs lead across to the trig point of The Cheviot at 815 metres. After descending very steeply from The Cheviot, make a beeline for Hedgehope Hill, the third highest peak in the Northumberland, before looping back to Wooler.

Low cloud is always a possibility here, so you should ensure that your navigation skills are up to scratch.

OTHER OPTIONS This route can be almost halved by starting in the Harthope Valley (road end near Langleeford Farm). Climb Scald Hill first and descend back to the start after Hedgehope Hill.

An easier and lower-level alternative is a linear route linking the Pennine Way and St Cuthbert's Way, which traverses the Cheviots from Kirk Yetholm to Wooler.

RACE The Chevy Chase event is organised by Wooler Running Club. The course is unmarked and runners can choose their own route, as long as the manned checkpoints are visited in the correct order and within the 6-hour cut-off.

The 88-kilometre Cheviot Goat ultra takes in much of this area and traditionally took place only in winter – though some years it is run in summer too, *www. cheviotgoat.com*

DISTANCE **31km** ASCENT **1,170m** TIME **5–6 hours**
START/FINISH **Wooler Youth Hostel** GRID REF **NT 991 277**
GPS **55.5436 , -2.0151** PUBLIC TRANSPORT **Wooler has good bus links with surrounding towns** PARKING **Ramsey Lane car park (free)**

WHAT NEXT? For similar challenge events try the Edale Skyline (see page 24), Tour de Helvellyn, Llangollen Hills, Ras y Moelwyn, the Ochil 2000s (see page 92) or the Pentland Skyline (see page 94). For something bigger but along similar lines, take a look at the Lyke Wake Walk on the North York Moors or the Fellsman in the Yorkshire Dales (see page 48).

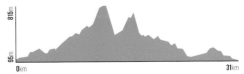

21

SENNEN COVE TO ST IVES

37km | **TRAIL** | **NAVIGATION** 1 fully waymarked
CORNWALL

Run one of the quietest and wildest sections
of the South West Coast Path – traversing high
cliffs, rugged headlands and narrow zawns
(inlets), while passing ruins that point to a
turbulent mining past.

DISTANCE **37km** ASCENT **720m** TIME **5:30–6:30 hours**
START **Sennen Cove** FINISH **St Ives** GRID REF **SW 354 263/SW 519 401**
GPS **50.0778, -5.6984/50.2095, -5.4777** PUBLIC TRANSPORT **Lengthy
bus connections are possible via Penzance - getting a lift is the best
option** PARKING **Various options at the start and finish (parking
charges apply)**

The beach resorts and small fishing villages of
the 'Cornish Riviera' are extremely busy in the
summer months. This is why the route from surfing
hotspot Sennen Cove to bustling St Ives is such
a gem. Rocky, boggy and sometimes demanding,
the feel is remote and the cliff views spectacular.
It is a challenge that gives a proper taste of the
rugged North Cornwall Coast and its heritage.

The route offers continuous interest, starting with
the beautiful Whitesand Bay, and a short section
of very easy scrambling before Porth Nanven, and
leading on to superb views at Cape Cornwall, where
the Gulf Stream splits. You'll pass numerous traces

of Cornwall's tin mining heritage, including stone
buildings and smoke stacks. The Levant Mine has
been restored by the National Trust. Leaping much
further back in time, Kenidjack Cliff Castle is one of
several Iron Age promontory forts along this coastline;
its ruins are perched above precipitous zawns.

While the granite cliffs of Bosigran make a dramatic
sight, tucked away amongst the cliffs there are many
rugged coves. The tiny sandy beach of Portheras
Cove, accessible only on foot, is a playground for seals,
as is the group of small rocky islands known as The
Carracks, while secluded Porthmeor Cove is a Site of
Special Scientific Interest, designated for its geology.
Compared to the wildness of most of this route,
the finish in busy St Ives is quite a contrast.

OTHER OPTIONS This route can be shortened by
starting at Zennor, which is accessible by bus
from St Ives. The next stretch (on to Hayle,
Portreath or St Agnes) boasts bigger sandy
beaches and more sea cliffs, but less ascent.

ULTRA ROUTE The South West Coast Path is England's
longest National Trail. The full route offers 1,014
kilometres of stunning trails around the entire South
West peninsula. There are numerous spectacular
sections of the trail, varying from sandy beaches, dunes
and cliffs to moorland, mines and picturesque fishing
villages. The South West Coast Path is linked along the
Devon/Cornwall border by the Tamara Coast to Coast
Way, so you can now do a complete 623-kilometre
circuit of Cornwall – the Kylgh Kernow.

RACE The Arc of Attrition, Roseland August Trail, the
Endurancelife Classic Quarter and the South West
Traverse all follow sections of the South West Coast
Path.

WHAT NEXT? Deservedly popular sections of the South West Coast Path include Newlyn to Land's End and the stunning Jurassic Coast in Dorset and Devon. For a little taster, try a loop around Lizard Point on the southern tip of Cornwall.

Other great coastal trails that can be tackled as sections or as fastpacking adventures are the Norfolk Coast Path; the Cleveland Way; Raad Ny Foillan on the Isle of Man; the Pembrokeshire Coast Path; the Moray Coast Trail; or the Kintyre Way.

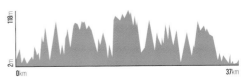

22

LANGDALE SKYLINE

32km | **MOUNTAIN** | **NAVIGATION** 4 difficult self-navigation or complex terrain
LAKE DISTRICT

A classic skyline challenge linking 12 spectacular rocky peaks in the heart of the Lake District National Park.

DISTANCE **32km** ASCENT **1,560m** TIME **6–7 hours** START/FINISH **Elterwater** GRID REF **NY 327 047** GPS **54.4341, -3.0375**
PUBLIC TRANSPORT **A few buses a day run to Elterwater from Kendal, via Windermere and Ambleside** PARKING **Elterwater National Trust car park (parking charges apply)**

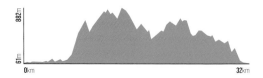

The Langdale Valley is breathtakingly beautiful and is located in the very heart of the Lake District National Park. The quaint village of Elterwater is an ideal base from which to link the impressive and much-loved Langdale Pikes in a technical traverse of the Langdale Skyline.

The route takes in 12 summits, but once you're at high level there is not as much descent and re-ascent as you might suppose. The round was first devised by Jack Emery (the English 2- and 3-mile record holder in the 1930s), who walked it in nine hours when in his 70s from his home in Chapel Stile.

A few short rock steps on the way up Pike of Blisco give a first taste of easy scrambling, before you head over Great Knott to Crinkle Crags (a line of minor rocky summits on Bow Fell's south ridge). The terrain here is complex and a real navigational challenge in poor visibility. The notorious 'Bad Step' is a short scramble on the highest crinkle. It looks worse than it is and there is an easier trail avoiding it to the left. Pass the Three Tarns to reach Bow Fell, then choose your preferred level of technicality for gaining Rossett Pike. After crossing boggy Martcrag Moor, you'll reach the rocky outcrops of the Langdale Pikes. Scramble up the cone of Pike of Stickle then across to Harrison Stickle (add Loft Crag too if you wish to be thorough). Follow the long ridge of Blea Rigg, taking vague paths over Great Castle How and on to Silver How before descending into Elterwater.

OTHER OPTIONS You can bypass Rossett Pike by taking a path to the north from Angle Tarn. Bypass the Langdale Pikes by crossing Martcrag Moor. Bail-out options include the Browney Gill path (from Red Tarn west of the Pike of Blisco), The Band (from Three Tarns), Rossett Gill (from Angle Tarn) or Stake Pass (from Langdale Combe).

A shorter version is the Langdale Horseshoe (Thunacar Knott, Esk Hause, Bow Fell and Crinkle Crags, finishing with the Pike of Blisco). For a short run, the Langdale Pikes can be linked in a short loop.

RACE The Langdale Horseshoe is a classic fell race organised annually by Ambleside AC. It starts and finishes at the Old Dungeon Ghyll and is part of the Lakeland Classics series. First held in 1973, it has one of the oldest course records in fell running history – the men's record has stood since 1977 (1:55.03 set by A. Styan). The women's record is 2:22.50 – it was set by V. Wilkinson in 2016.

WHAT NEXT? For other big rounds, try the Cairngorm 4000s (see page 108); the Waun Fach Horseshoe in the Black Mountains; the Ennerdale Horseshoe or the Mosedale Horseshoe in the Lake District; the Glen Shiel Skyline; the Ring of Steall (see page 82); or the super-remote Fisherfield Munros.

N
0   1 Km

Sergeant Man ▲

Easedale Tarn

Esk Pike ▲   Angle   Rossett Pike
                   Tarn

                                    Pike of   Stickle Tarn   GRASMERE ●
                                    Stickle ▲   Harrison Stickle

Bow Fell ▲   Silver How

Crinkle   Grasmere
Crags

                                    Side Pike ▲   CHAPEL
Long Top ▲   STILE

Great Knott ▲   Pike   Lingmoor   ELTERWATER
                  of Blisco   Fell ▲   Ⓢ

                                    Blea Tarn

         Red Tarn   Elter Water

© JOHN COEFIELD

© JOHN COEFIELD

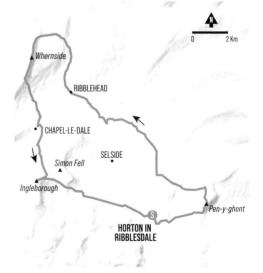

Whernside

RIBBLEHEAD

CHAPEL-LE-DALE

Simon Fell

SELSIDE

Ingleborough

Pen-y-ghent

HORTON IN
RIBBLESDALE

0   2 Km

23

YORKSHIRE THREE PEAKS

39km | **TRAIL** | **NAVIGATION** 2 partial waymarking
YORKSHIRE DALES

Traverse the peaks of Pen-y-ghent, Whernside and Ingleborough as fast as you can!

| DISTANCE **39km** ASCENT **1,400m** TIME **5:45–6:45 hours**
| START/FINISH **Horton in Ribblesdale** GRID REF **SD 807 726**
| GPS **54.1497, -2.2960** PUBLIC TRANSPORT **Regular trains from**
| **Horton in Ribblesdale** PARKING **Horton in Ribblesdale car park**
| **(parking charges apply)**

Every year, thousands of people visit the Yorkshire Dales to climb one – or all – of the Three Peaks. This classic circular is the oldest challenge in the national park and was originally devised for walkers, who must complete the round in under 12 hours by a circular route, starting and finishing at the same point. For runners, the aim is simply to complete in the minimum time possible.

There are three usual start points (Chapel-le-Dale, Horton in Ribblesdale or Ribblehead) – here we describe the route from Horton in Ribblesdale.

From Horton in Ribblesdale, climb the steep southern side of Pen-y-ghent and descend to the north, which is gentler. From here, you head north to Ribblehead, admiring the spectacular viaduct en route and crossing the railway by a small aqueduct along Little Dale. Admire the Force Gill waterfall as you ascend towards Grain Head, and up to the top of Whernside, the tallest of the Three Peaks at 736 metres. From Whernside there's a steep descent to Bruntscar Farm. After passing Chapel-le-Dale, the trail follows limestone pavements, slabs and wooden boards over Humphrey Bottom and the Ingleborough National Nature Reserve, before climbing to the Ingleborough summit plateau. From here, descend Simon Fell Breast, passing limestone outcrops Sulber and Sulber Nick, to return to Horton in Ribblesdale.

OTHER OPTIONS For a shorter challenge, any of the Three Peaks can be tackled in isolation.

ULTRA ROUTE The 70-kilometre Yorkshire 3 Peaks Ultra has an optional bonus 30-kilometre loop at the end for those wishing to complete a 'metric century' (time limits apply), *www.rangerultras.co.uk*

© STEPHEN ROSS

RACE Described as 'the marathon with mountains', the Three Peaks Race originated in 1954 (starting in Chapel-le-Dale) with only six starters and three finishers. Course records are (F) Victoria Wilkinson at 3:09.19 in 2017 and (M) Andy Peace at 2:46.03 in 1996). *www.threepeaksrace.org*

WHAT NEXT? Other peak bagging rounds include the Surrey Three Peaks or the Edale Skyline (see page 24). There's also the National Three Peaks, the Welsh Three Peaks or the Scottish 4000s challenges, which involve a drive, cycle or very long run between summits.

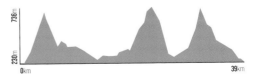

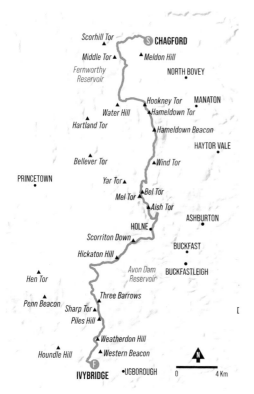

24
CHAGFORD TO IVYBRIDGE

50km | **TRAIL** | **NAVIGATION** 1 fully waymarked
DEVON

The most rugged section of the Two Moors Way; a remote journey weaving through the medieval villages, sculpted tors and tumbling rivers of Dartmoor National Park.

DISTANCE **50km** ASCENT **1,110m** TIME **6:30-7:30 hours** START **Chagford** FINISH **Ivybridge** GRID REF **SX 701 874/SX 640 567** GPS **50.6723, -3.8391/50.3948, -3.9136** PUBLIC TRANSPORT **A few buses per day run between Exeter and Moretonhampstead via Chagford. Direct trains run between Ivybridge and Exeter** PARKING **Various options in Chagford and Ivybridge (parking charges apply)**

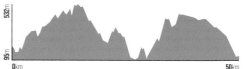

25
DERWENT WATERSHED

69km | **FELL** | **NAVIGATION** 4 difficult self-navigation or complex terrain
PEAK DISTRICT

A sometimes pathless, high-level route around the Derwent Watershed in the Dark Peak.

DISTANCE **69km** ASCENT **1,600m** TIME **8-10 hours** START/FINISH **Edale** GRID REF **SK 123 852** GPS **53.3643, -1.8155** PUBLIC TRANSPORT **Regular trains between Sheffield and Manchester Piccadilly stop at Edale** PARKING **Edale car park (parking charges apply)**

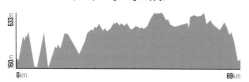

This challenge takes you over some of the Peak District's highest hills and most deserted areas of moorland, including Lose Hill, Win Hill, Back Tor, Bleaklow, Kinder Scout and Brown Knoll, just sidestepping Mam Tor. It is regarded as a classic by walkers and fell runners alike (sadly, the High Peak Marathon – which followed the watershed route – hasn't run for several years), and is based on a long-distance walk reputed to have been established in 1918 by Eustace Thomas of the Manchester Rucksack Club.

From Edale, a steep climb leads up Hollins Cross then on to Lose Hill. Descend to cross the River Noe and head back up Win Hill on the other side of the valley. The route loses height again to cross the River Derwent, then climbs up to the famous gritstone rocks of Stanage Edge, passing High Neb and heading along to Derwent Edge. A trail leads along the Cartledge Stones Ridge, then down to Howden Edge. The section over Howden Moors largely consists of leg-sapping featureless bog-trotting across a landscape of groughs. Just after Bleaklow, the route joins the Pennine Way and progress improves dramatically. From here it is

The Two Moors Way links Exmoor with Dartmoor, crossing the quiet countryside of Mid Devon in between. The section from Chagford to Ivybridge best captures the bewitching landscape of Dartmoor with its granite tors, charming hamlets and Bronze Age archaeology. Watch out for Dartmoor ponies along the way.

From the attractive market town of Chagford, head west to join the Two Moors Way, linking the interestingly named Teigncombe, Great Frenchbeer, Teignworthy and Yardworthy, then crossing the B3212 near Bennett's Cross, a 13th-century boundary marker. Next up is 497-metre Hookney Tor, a striking granite outcrop, beyond which the trail drops down to Grimspound. The 24 hut circles and boundary wall here comprise the best-preserved Bronze Age settlement on Dartmoor. The route continues south to the village of Holne.

From Holne, the way runs west to Scorriton, Hickaton Hill and then Huntingdon Warren. You'll cross the River Avon on a 19th-century clapper bridge and finally pick up the old Redlake Tramway through barren Ugborough Moor before finishing at Ivybridge.

OTHER OPTIONS Extend by finishing at Yealmpton or add on the adjacent sections of the Way (Lynmouth to Chagford or Ivybridge to Wembury). If staying in the area, run though the wooded valleys of Lustleigh Cleave, Wistman's Wood or Fingle Gorge. To start tor-bagging try Haytor Rocks and Hound Tor. The highest tors on Dartmoor are the adjacent Yes Tor (619 metres) and High Willhays (621 metres).

ULTRA ROUTE The Two Moors Way is a 164-kilometre trail stretching from Lynmouth on the North Devon coast to Ivybridge on the southern border of Dartmoor. To complete a coast-to-coast run, carry on to Wembury on the South Devon coast, which adds on 24 kilometres. The FKTs for the full Two Moors Way are (F) Laura Swanton-Rouvelin at 1:01:12.00 in 2019 and (M) James Graham at 22:51.59 in 2022.

RACE The Race with No Name (Dartmoor Traverse East to West) runs from Trenchford Reservoir to Tavistock (50 kilometres). There are also the Dartmoor in a Day events (30- and 50-kilometre versions), the Devon Coast to Coast Ultra Marathon and The Crossing.

WHAT NEXT? For much bigger challenges consider the Dartmoor Way (174 kilometres) or the tor-bagging Dartmoor Round (120 kilometres). For similar landscape, try moorland sections of the Pennine Way, Limestone Way or the Cleveland Way. Alternatively, enter the Hardmoors Race Series in North Yorkshire.

---

a lovely run along the flagstones of Mill Hill and past Kinder Downfall, then south to Rushup Edge, around Mam Tor and back to Hollins Cross and Edale.

GOOD TO KNOW This route is based on the High Peak Marathon – a classic race with a long history, now sadly defunct due to difficulties with access on the race route. Nicky Spinks has set up a new race – Bruce's Crown – which is due to premiere in 2024 in the Galloway Hills; it is inspired by the High Peak Marathon and its history, www.brucescrown.co.uk

OTHER OPTIONS The route is bisected by the Snake Pass (A57), so can be completed over two consecutive days for an easier undertaking. There are many intersecting trails throughout, which can provide escape routes as required.

WHAT NEXT? Other great challenges include the Grampian Mountain Challenge, the OMM (Original Mountain Marathon), the Hardmoors Race Series in North Yorkshire, the Montane Cheviot Goat, the Fellsman in the Yorkshire Dales (see page 48); the Edale Skyline

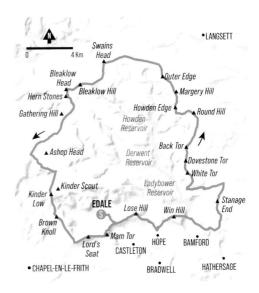

(see page 24) and the Dovedale Dipper. Or go big with the Montane Spine Race!

26

GEORGE FISHER'S TEA ROUND

47km | FELL | NAVIGATION 4 difficult self-navigation or complex terrain
LAKE DISTRICT

Tick off the ten tops you can see from the warmth of the cafe at George Fisher in Keswick.

DISTANCE **47km**   ASCENT **2,930m**   TIME **7–10 hours**
RECORDS **(F) Fi Pascall 6:02.47 in 2022; (M) Brennan Townshend**
4:44.00 in 2021   START/FINISH **George Fisher store, Keswick**
GRID REF **NY 266 232**   GPS **54.5992, -3.1364**   PUBLIC TRANSPORT
Bus links with the surrounding towns and villages   PARKING
Various options in Keswick (parking charges apply)

This ingenious round was devised in 2017 by Jacob Tonkin, who worked at the George Fisher outdoor shop in Keswick (once the famous Abraham brothers' photographic shop) and proposed linking the fells he could see from the window of the cafe on the shop's top floor. Since its inception the popularity of the route has soared, and the challenge has attracted many of the big names in British fell running. To be added to the leader board, record your time door-to-door using a smartwatch or app. Finishers receive a Tea Round

badge and a T-shirt. For more information, visit *www.georgefisher.co.uk/tearound*

You can run the challenge clockwise or anticlockwise; either way this is a fantastic place to start for people looking to explore endurance mountain running, taking in some of the finest views in the country.

OTHER OPTIONS   If this is a bit long, try the 23-kilometre Espresso Round which has just four summits – Cat Bells, Rowling End, Causey Pike and Barrow.

RACE   There are plenty of great options in the vicinity, including the Grisedale Grind, the Darren Holloway Memorial Race (Buttermere Horseshoe), the Causey Pike fell race and the Barrow fell race.

WHAT NEXT?   For something similar try the Cambrian Traverse, the Lunar Round, the Mountain Goat, the Yorkshire Three Peaks (see page 35), the Llangollen Fell Race (see page 146), the Pentland Skyline (see page 94) or the remote Paps of Jura (see page 78). For a bigger challenge, take on the mighty Bob Graham Round (see page 48).

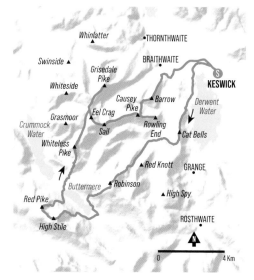

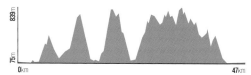

27

OLD COUNTY TOPS FELL RACE

57km | **FELL** | **NAVIGATION** 4 difficult self-navigation or complex terrain
LAKE DISTRICT

A classic Lakeland fell race linking Helvellyn, Scafell Pike and the Old Man of Coniston.

DISTANCE **57km**   ASCENT **2,850m**   TIME **7–10 hours**
START/FINISH **New Dungeon Ghyll Hotel, Langdale**   GRID REF **NY 295 064**
GPS **54.4483, -3.0874**   PUBLIC TRANSPORT **Buses run from Ambleside to New Dungeon Ghyll**   PARKING **New Dungeon Ghyll car park (parking charges apply)**

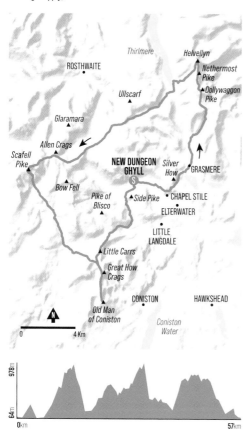

Helvellyn, Scafell Pike and the Old Man of Coniston are the traditional county tops of Westmorland, Cumberland and Lancashire respectively. The Old County Tops Fell Race summits them in an anticlockwise round, visiting the following checkpoints in order: New Dungeon Ghyll Hotel, path junction underneath Seat Sandal (NY 339 098), Helvellyn, Wythburn car park, Angle Tarn, Scafell Pike, Cockley Beck, Old Man of Coniston, the Three Shire Stone (NY 277 027) and back to the New Dungeon Ghyll Hotel.

This is a historic race but can also be completed in your own time. Unmarked (even on race day), you can take any permissible line between checkpoints, so the exact distance and ascent depends on the line you take. The challenge is legendary: there are bogs, tussocks, wild descents and steep climbs, stretching the definition of 'runnable' to its utmost.

From the New Dungeon Ghyll Hotel, pick your own route over trail and fell to Grasmere, then find a way up to Hause Gap and along the massif of Dollywaggon Pike, Nethermost Pike and Helvellyn. From the summit of Helvellyn, descend Middle Tongue, then head up Wyth Burn – trying not to be swallowed by the relent-

LEFT © STEPHEN WILSON www.granddayoutphotography.co.uk. RIGHT © KIRSTY READE

less deep bog – and along Greenup Edge, aiming for Angle Tarn. Now head for Esk Hause, skirting past Ill Crag and Broad Crag to join the tourist track up to the summit of Scafell Pike at 978 metres.

It's up to you whether you choose the gentler descent or the 'straight off the edge' option down to the hamlet of Cockley Beck, but then there's *only* one more monstrous climb up Grey Friar before the flatter out-and-back to the summit of The Old Man of Coniston. Descend to Wrynose Pass and the Three Shire Stone (marking the conjunction of the old counties of Lancashire, Cumberland and Westmorland) and then all that remains is to return via Blea Tarn to Langdale.

OTHER OPTIONS

Each of the Old County Tops is a great hill run in its own right. Helvellyn can be climbed in numerous ways and can be spiced up by including the scrambles along Striding and Swirral edges (see page 11).

Scafell Pike has a busy tourist route but if you're looking for something different, approach via the Corridor Route from Borrowdale or Seathwaite.

A great way to run the 'Old Man' is to jog up past The Bell and through the quarries to the summit, descending via Swirl How and past Levers Water. Finish down through the Coppermines Valley.

RACE The Old County Tops Fell Race is a pairs race organised by the Achille Ratti Climbing Club. The race was first held in 1988 and has been held almost every year since. The course records are (F) Lisa Watson and Despina Berdini at 7:51.18 in 2023, (M) Rob Jebb and Ricky Lightfoot at 6:21.00 in 2018, and (mixed) Caitlin Rice and Tim Budd at 7:43.12 in 2015 – winners receive a coveted mug. For more information or to enter, visit *www.achille-ratti-climbing-club.co.uk*

WHAT NEXT? The Dungeon Ghyll and Grisedale Horseshoe fell races are also organised by the Achille Ratti Climbing Club. Other Lakeland classics include the Ennerdale Horseshoe, the Darren Holloway Memorial Race (Buttermere Horseshoe), the Langdale Skyline (see page 32), the Three Shires Fell Race or the Borrowdale Fell Race. You could also try the Fellsman in the nearby Yorkshire Dales (see page 48).

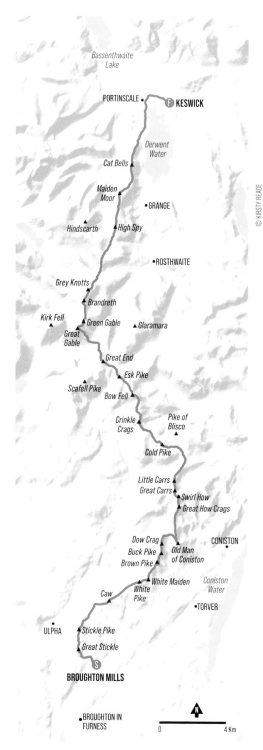

© KIRSTY READE

28

CUMBRIAN TRAVERSE

50km | **FELL** | **NAVIGATION 4** difficult self-navigation or complex terrain
LAKE DISTRICT

A high-level traverse of 21 Lakeland peaks – this is a great introduction to the bigger fell running challenges of the Lake District.

DISTANCE **50km**   ASCENT **2,860m**   TIME **7-10 hours**
START **Broughton Mills**   FINISH **Keswick**   GRID REF **SD 222 907/NY 266 234**
GPS **54.3061, -3.1966/54.6007, -3.1371**   PUBLIC TRANSPORT **No practical options**   PARKING **There is a small car park in Broughton Mills opposite the village hall – please park considerately. Various options in Keswick (parking charges apply)**

The Cumbrian Traverse marks an aesthetically pleasing line on the map, striking a bold line south to north through the Lake District and seeking out the highest ridges and summits. It was first devised by Sue and Dick Courchee in 2005 and was intended as an informal outing without time limits. The route takes in 21 fabulous Lakeland peaks, including the popular summits of the Old Man of Coniston, Crinkle Crags, Bow Fell and Great Gable. Details of completions and

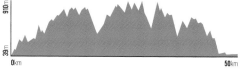

© MARTYN PRICE

© KIRSTY READE

how to register your traverse are available at *gofar997. wixsite.com/gofar/cumbrian-traverse*

It starts off with good running amid the little-known gems of the Dunnerdale Fells, then heads for the big hitters (via a grassy climb up White Maiden), with Dow Crag and the Old Man of Coniston up first. Next is a runnable ridge towards Swirl How, heading over the Great Carrs and Little Carrs before descending to the Wrynose Pass and the Three Shire Stone.

There are great views of the Duddon Valley and Eskdale on the way up Cold Pike, then the complex tops of Crinkle Crags entice you north towards the summit of Bow Fell. Down at Sty Head, you are confronted by the giant bulk of Great Gable, but once conquered, there's good running over Green Gable, Brandreth and Grey Knotts, before descending to the Honister Pass.

It is relatively easy going from High Spy along the ridge to Maiden Moor and the busy summit of Cat Bells, the final peak on the challenge, so you can glory in the fantastic views of Derwent Water and your destination of Keswick. The official finish is to touch the doors of the famous Moot Hall.

OTHER OPTIONS You can bail out most easily at Wrynose Pass or the Honister Pass. You can also retreat to Langdale from Three Tarns (via The Band) or to Wasdale or Seathwaite from Styhead Tarn.

RACE Many classic fell races pass near sections of this route, including the Coniston Fell Race, the Langdale Skyline (see page 32), the Great Lakes Fell Race, the Old County Tops Fell Race (see page 40) and the Borrowdale Fell Race.

WHAT NEXT? Similar challenges in the Lake District include the Joss Naylor Lakeland Challenge (originally aimed at over-50s but now with a range of time allowances), the Lakeland 3000s or George Fisher's Tea Round (see page 38). The five legs of the well-known Bob Graham Round (see page 48) are excellent challenges in their own right and are a good way of building up from shorter fell running challenges to the ultimate Lakeland 24-hour round. Elsewhere you might consider the Yorkshire Three Peaks (see page 35), the Welsh 3000s (see page 156) or the Lochaber Traverse (see page 104).

29
BAY LIMESTONE ROUND

90km | TRAIL | NAVIGATION 4 difficult self-navigation or complex terrain
CUMBRIA AND LANCASHIRE

An exploratory challenge linking 13 limestone summits around picturesque Morecambe Bay.

DISTANCE **90km**   ASCENT **1,810m**   TIME **11–13 hours**   START **Kents Bank railway station**   FINISH **Arnside Pier**   GRID REF **SD 396 756/SD 456 788**   GPS **54.1728, -2.9253/54.2024, -2.8352**   PUBLIC TRANSPORT **Arnside railway station is a short walk from the pier at the end of the route, from where it is a short but scenic train journey back to Kents Bank**   PARKING **Various options in Kents Bank and Arnside**

This round was created by fell runners Tom Phillips and Penny Attwood as a lockdown challenge in 2020. It can be completed solo or as a team relay and challengers are required to raise money for charity. To be included in the Roll of Honour, notify the overseers beforehand via the official website: *www.bay-limestone-round.org.uk*

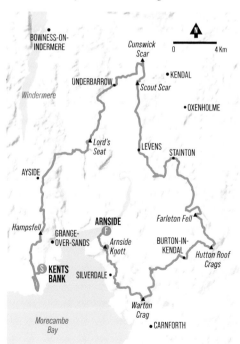

The innovative route links the cairns surrounding Morecambe Bay: Humphrey Head, Hampsfell, Lord's Seat, Cunswick Scar, Scout Scar, Heversham Head, Farleton Knott, Hutton Roof Crags, Cringlebarrow, Heald Brow, King William's Hill and Arnside Knott.

The route is prescriptive due to certain hazards and to protect the environment – going wrong will earn you a disqualification. A thorough route description and GPX file are available from the website. The challenge is trickier than it looks with so many tiny and sometimes obscure tops to seek out, so it is well worth having a recce first.

OTHER OPTIONS Individual sections of the round make great linear routes in their own right. Another option is to run the final hilly section from Heversham Head to Arnside, and either get a lift to complete the route or run as a smaller loop.

RACE The 10-kilometre Arnside Knott Race takes place each November, *www.arnsideknott.blogspot.com*

WHAT NEXT? Try George Fisher's Tea Round (see page 38), the Derwent Watershed (see page 36), a round in the Cheviot Hills, or one of the Northern Traverse events. For something shorter try the Espresso Round (see page 38), Pentland Skyline (see page 94) or the Old County Tops Fell Race (see page 40). If it's obscure top-bagging that you enjoy, why not hunt out some tricky tors on the longer Dartmoor Round.

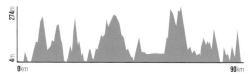

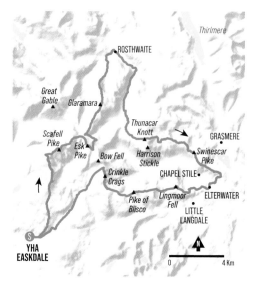

GERRY CHARNLEY ROUND

62km | **FELL** | **NAVIGATION** 4 difficult self-navigation
or complex terrain
LAKE DISTRICT

A commemorative fell running challenge and
a unique collection of interlinked circuits in
the Lake District – devised to celebrate the late
Gerry Charnley.

HARDMOORS 55

86km | **FELL** | **NAVIGATION** 1 fully waymarked
NORTH YORKSHIRE

The Hardmoors 55 event is a tough, often
wintery, 55-mile ultramarathon, passing
through the rugged North York Moors and
neighbouring Cleveland Hills.

DISTANCE **86km**   ASCENT **1,910m**   TIME **9–12 hours**   START **Guisborough**
FINISH **Helmsley**   GRID REF **NZ 616 154/SE 610 843**   GPS **54.5304, -1.0486/
54.2509, -1.0650**   PUBLIC TRANSPORT **Guisborough and Helmsley have
good bus links with surrounding towns. On race day, a coach
(pre-bookings only) takes competitors from the finish to the start,
before the event**   PARKING **Various options in Guisborough and
Helmsley**

A tough race across wild countryside, with wintery
conditions to boot. However, reliable waymarking
makes this challenge a good starting point for those
looking to test their self-reliance in a vast moorland
landscape renowned for heavy snowfall.

The route starts at Guisborough, joining the Cleveland

Way National Trail just outside the town. There is
good waymarking through Guisborough Woods and
on to North Yorkshire's most famous hill, Roseberry
Topping (which has excellent views for its relatively
modest 320-metre height). As the route heads into the
Cleveland Hills, there's good running along easy trails,
passing Captain Cook's Monument, followed by a fun
descent to Kildale. Then it's back uphill to the Three
Sisters (Wainstones via the flagstone path, then Cold
Moor and Cringle Moor). These are rolling moorland
hills, requiring a series of steep rocky climbs followed
by technical downhill sections.

Once you reach Osmotherley, there's another climb
out of the village back up to the plateau, but there's
good running to Sutton Bank, where there's an out
and back (3-kilometre round trip) to the White Horse,
the UK's most northerly hill figure, which was made
in 1857. Walk the steep steps here to give your legs a
break! From here it's not far to the outskirts of Helmsley,
where a stone marks the end of the Cleveland Way, and
there's an ice cream shop, though the Hardmoors 55
route continues to Helmsley Sports Club.

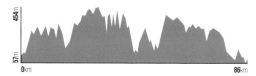

DISTANCE **62km** ASCENT **3,200m** TIME **10:30–12:30 hours**
START/FINISH **Anywhere**

Gerry Charnley is credited with having brought the sport of orienteering to England and jointly organised the UK's first mountain marathon in 1968. Sadly, he was killed in a tragic accident in the Lakeland fells in 1982, after which the Gerry Charnley Round (originally known as the Gerry Charnley Way) was created in his memory by the South Ribble Orienteering Club.

Any start location and direction of travel is permitted but all of the 26 controls should be visited in a closed loop. The full round is comprised of three shorter circuits, which can be linked together or tackled as independent challenges – or even as part of a relay. Each of the circuits starts at a different youth hostel but all visit the Charnley Crag Cairn, south of Esk Pike (NY 236 070). This commemorative cairn is marked with a memorial plaque, placed by the orienteering club.

As in any orienteering style event, there is no prescribed route for this challenge; runners devise their own line between controls. A suggested order of controls is given (with grid references) on the official commemorative Harvey map, starting and finishing at Eskdale Youth Hostel.

OTHER OPTIONS The three component circuits – Eskdale, Borrowdale and Langdale – are excellent objectives in their own right and make this challenge accessible to more runners.

RACE There are many popular fell races in this area, including the Great Lakes Fell Race, Borrowdale Fell Race and the Langdale Skyline (see page 32) – or, for something shorter, the Blisco Dash.

WHAT NEXT? For other orienteering style events in the mountains, try the OMM (Original Mountain Marathon), the Hodgson Brothers Mountain Relay, the Saunders Lakeland Mountain Marathon, the Great Lakeland 3Day or the Grampian Mountain Challenge.

OTHER OPTIONS There are many circular trails that can be linked with the Cleveland Way. There are some ideas at *www.nationaltrail.co.uk/en_GB/trails/cleveland-way*

ULTRA ROUTE The 175-kilometre Cleveland Way National Trail circumnavigates the North York Moors from Helmsley to Filey Brigg, combining rugged moorland with beautiful coastline. Most people completing the full trail go in a clockwise direction, but the challenge below is run anticlockwise.

RACE There are nine Hardmoors ultra events (including the Hardmoors 55) and six trail races based around the North York Moors and the Cleveland Hills. For more information or to enter, see *www.hardmoors110.org.uk*

WHAT NEXT? For the diehards there are a number of challenges which involve collecting Hardmoors completions – including the Triple Ring Challenge, Super Slam and the Hardmoors 1000 mile Club. The longest of the Hardmoors events is the Hardmoors 200 (Kingston upon Hull to Helmsley).

For a range of other moorland adventures consider the Derwent Watershed (see page 36), the Two Moors Way, Montane Cheviot Goat or the Fellsman (see page 48). For a solo challenge in the same area, try the Lyke Wake Walk.

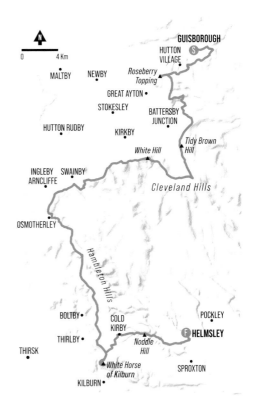

32
THE FELLSMAN

97km | **FELL** | **NAVIGATION 4** difficult self-navigation or complex terrain
YORKSHIRE DALES

This iconic fell race comprises a high-level traverse across harsh and rugged moorland.

DISTANCE **97km** ASCENT **3,460m** TIME **13–16 hours** RECORDS **(F)**
Jasmin Paris 11:09.00 in 2015; (M) Jez Bragg 10:06.00 in 2011
START **Ingleton** FINISH **Threshfield** GRID REF **SD 694 730/SD 993 639**
GPS **54.1519, -2.4700/54.0710, -2.0121** PUBLIC TRANSPORT **Ingleton and
Threshfield have good bus links** PARKING **Free parking at Threshfield
and bus transport to the start is provided by the race organiser**

The Fellsman is a classic Yorkshire race, which first took place in 1962 in the opposite direction to the current race. Most of the Fellsman route is on privately owned land, so race access has to be negotiated annually. Recceing the route on any other occasion is prohibited and could jeopardise the future of the event.

Starting from the village of Ingleton, the route explores the Yorkshire Dales, taking in numerous summits en route. Don't be tempted to start up Ingleborough too quickly – there's a very long way to go from here and the descent is rocky. Next up is Whernside, after which you're off the beaten track and need to start concentrating on the navigation. There's a hefty climb up Gragareth, the second highest point in modern Lancashire, then it's over Great Coum and down into the picturesque Dales

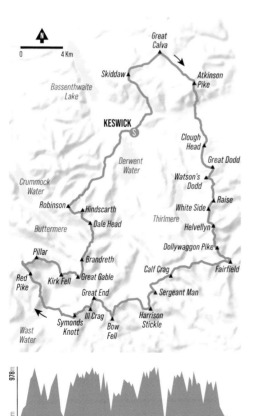

33
BOB GRAHAM ROUND

103km | **FELL** | **NAVIGATION 4** difficult self-navigation or complex terrain
LAKE DISTRICT

The most well-known 24-hour mountain round in the UK – a classic loop of 42 summits in the Lake District.

DISTANCE **103km** ASCENT **6,870m** TIME **21–24 hours**
RECORDS **(F) Beth Pascall 14:34.00 in 2020; (M) Jack Keunzle 12:23.00
in 2022** START/FINISH **Moot Hall, Keswick** GRID REF **NY 266 234**
GPS **54.6004, -3.1376** PUBLIC TRANSPORT **Keswick has good bus links
with surrounding towns and villages** PARKING **Various options in
Keswick for overnight parking, including Keswick Rugby Club (parking
charges apply)**

The Bob Graham Round was first conceived when the round's namesake broke the Lake District 24-hour fell record by traversing 42 peaks within 24 hours in June 1932. The round was not repeated until Alan Heaton did so in 1960, but since then it has seen over 2,500 registered completions (and a great many more that have gone unrecorded).

village of Dent (technically located in Cumbria).

The route traverses Blea Moor then drops back into Dentdale at Stone House, visiting the 11-arch Arten Gill Viaduct (built of 'Dent marble', actually a dark limestone), before climbing Great Knoutberry Hill. Snaizeholme Fell, Dodd Fell and boggy Middle Tongue follow. The final leg runs across the hills east of Wharfedale, then drops down into the village of Grassington, crossing the river Wharfe to reach Threshfield.

The terrain is challenging and featureless and the route does not follow waymarked or well-trodden footpaths so navigational skills are essential, particularly in clag and at night. Competitors plot their own route between the 26 checkpoints, but there are areas where a strict route must be adhered to:

details are available on the event website and are strictly enforced. The use of GPS devices is permitted.

OTHER OPTIONS For something much shorter in the Dales, try the Yorkshire Three Peaks (see page 35).

RACE The event is open to both walkers and runners, as long as they meet the timing limits, and is legendary for its smorgasbord of checkpoint food, *www.fellsman.org.uk*

WHAT NEXT? Other events with a similar feel include the Montane Spine Race, the Cheviot Goat and the various Hardmoors events (see page 46). If you're looking for your first ultra on moorland, you might try The Dartmoor Crossing or the Race with No Name.

In 2018, visiting Catalan runner Kilian Jornet made waves by completing the round in 12 hours and 52 minutes, breaking the long-standing record belonging to Billy Bland of 13 hours and 53 minutes, which had stood for 36 years. Since then, the standard has remained high with Scottish runner Finlay Wild nipping at Kilian's heels, finishing just 7 minutes behind in 2021. The following year the record was broken again by visiting US runner and accomplished FKT artist Jack Keunzle. The female record is just as breathtaking, with British trail runner Beth Pascall taking a huge 49 minutes off the talented fell runner Jasmin Paris in 2020.

The route takes in 42 summits in a circular round, including the popular Lakeland summits of Skiddaw, Blencathra, Helvellyn, Fairfield, Bow Fell, Scafell Pike and Great Gable. It is widely regarded as the easiest (and most runnable) of Great Britain's Big Three mountain rounds.

To become a member of the official Bob Graham 24 Hour Club, attempts must be registered with the membership secretary ahead of time and completed with pacers/support on the hill. Unsupported or commercially guided rounds are not recognised. There is a clear set of ethics and a strong sense of tradition surrounding 'the Bob' which sits at the beating heart of the fell running community.

GOOD TO KNOW Due to the dramatic increase in the popularity of the Bob Graham Round it is recommended that you consider the environmental impact of your round by limiting the numbers of pacers and recces, and considering your route choice carefully wherever possible to minimise erosion.

OTHER OPTIONS The five legs of the Bob Graham Round make great linear routes in their own right – or you could get creative and extend each leg to form a loop.

RACE As with all classic long rounds, this route takes in several summits that are the routes of established fell races. Examples include Scafell Pike, Dale Head, the Langdale Skyline, the Fairfield Horseshoe, Steel Fell, Skiddaw and Seat Sandal.

WHAT NEXT? If you've completed the Bob Graham Round, then the obvious next step is one of Great Britain's other Big Three mountain rounds: the Paddy Buckley Round (see page 164) or the Charlie Ramsay Round (see page 114). For something a little different, try the 26 Lake, Meres and Waters challenge. For easier local alternatives, try George Fisher's Tea Round (see page 38), the Cumbrian Traverse (see page 42) or the Gerry Charnley Round (see page 46).

34
OFFROAD JOGLE

over 1,400km | **TRAIL** | **NAVIGATION 3** no waymarking
GREAT BRITAIN

A trail-linking, route-planning, ultrarunning bonanza; complete the ultimate linear challenge by running the length of Great Britain from John o' Groats to Land's End, your way.

| DISTANCE **over 1,400km** ASCENT **variable** TIME **2 weeks–3 months**
| START **John o' Groats** FINISH **Land's End**

The oldest and most definitive journey along the length of Britain – a mind-bending challenge with tons of potential for innovation. The first recorded walk from John o' Groats to Land's End was undertaken by the brothers John and Robert Naylor in 1871. Since then, it has grown hugely in popularity and is now a timeless bucket-list challenge for anyone with a screw loose and a penchant for extremely sore feet.

There is no continuous long-distance trail from John o' Groats to Land's End. There are, however, recognised long-distance routes and National Trails which can be linked together. These can in turn be creatively connected by rights of way and minor roads. Many alternative routes exist and there is plenty of scope for personalising this lengthy adventure. Although the challenge can be completed in reverse (i.e. Land's End to John o' Groats – LEJOG), most prefer to run north to south to make use of weather windows on the most demanding sections through the Scottish Highlands.

Walkers typically take 2–3 months for this expedition. The records for running LEJOG by road belong to (F) Carla Molinaro in 12:00:30.14 in 2020 and (M) Dan Lawson in 9:21:14.02 in 2020. In 2009, ultrarunner Kevin Carr completed the challenge solo and unsupported in 6 weeks 3 days and 17 hours (including three rest days). His route was 2,018 kilometres in length and around 80 per cent off-road. The first female runner to complete the challenge was Marie-Claire Oziem in 2014, who also ran solo and unsupported, on a mixture of road and trail.

What better way to cross two (or possibly three) countries and explore some of Great Britain's best long-distance trails as you go?

© SHUTTERSTOCK/DAVID SANCHEZ PEREZ

OTHER OPTIONS Can you think of a spin on this classic challenge? In 2014, a team of four high-profile adventurers made the journey in a straight line over 28 days. The charity challenge, which became known as the Beeline Britain, involved two huge sea-kayak crossings, cycling and hiking along a direct route that even included the summit of Ben Macdui in the Cairngorms. 'Straight-line challenges' are a type of adventure challenge in their own right with the most recent of note being The Longest Line by Jenny Graham and Calum Maclean in 2021. The pair followed the longest straight line in the UK without crossing a road, which covered 71.5 kilometres of rough ground in the Cairngorms.

RACE Incredibly, JOGLE is organised as a road race by Ultrarunning Ltd (competitor numbers are limited to just 10 people), *www.ultrarunningltd.co.uk/race/jogle*, or you could do LEJOG as a more trail-oriented challenge by Rat Race, *www.ratrace.com/run-britannia*

WHAT NEXT? There are currently 16 National Trails in England and Wales and 29 Great Trails in Scotland. Once complete, the King Charles III England Coast Path will be the 17th in England and the longest in Great Britain at 4,350 kilometres. Other worthy but shorter alternatives for going extra-long include the Scottish National Trail (864 kilometres across Scotland from Kirk Yetholm to Cape Wrath) or the South West Coast Path (1,014 kilometres).

PREVIOUS SPREAD © © JON BARTON. OPPOSITE © ROSS BRANNIGAN

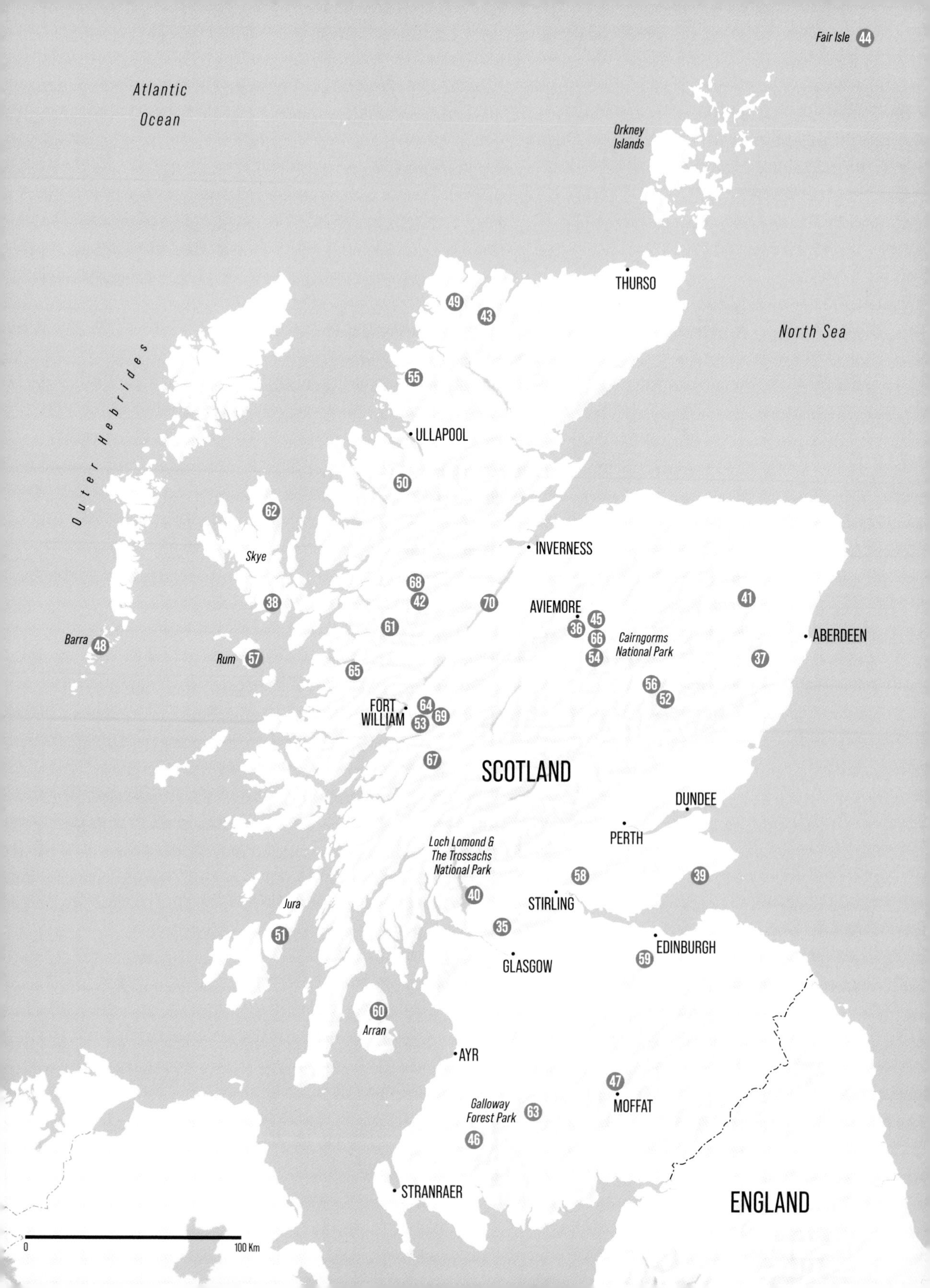

Fair Isle 44
Atlantic Ocean
Orkney Islands
THURSO
49
43
North Sea
Outer Hebrides
55
ULLAPOOL
50
62
INVERNESS
Skye
68
42
70
AVIEMORE
45
41
38
36
66
Cairngorms National Park
ABERDEEN
61
Barra 48
Rum 57
54
37
65
56
52
FORT WILLIAM
64
69
53
67
SCOTLAND
DUNDEE
PERTH
Loch Lomond & The Trossachs National Park
58
39
40
STIRLING
Jura
35
51
EDINBURGH
GLASGOW
59
60
Arran
AYR
47
MOFFAT
Galloway Forest Park
63
46
STRANRAER
ENGLAND
0
100 Km

SCOTLAND

35 **Mugdock Country Park**
5km | TRAIL | NAVIGATION **1**

36 **Loch an Eilein**
5km | TRAIL | NAVIGATION **2**

37 **Crathes Castle Parkrun**
5km | TRAIL | NAVIGATION **1**

38 **Loch Coruisk**
7km | TRAIL | NAVIGATION **3**

39 **Lower Largo to Elie**
11km | TRAIL | NAVIGATION **1**

40 **Conic Hill**
5km | TRAIL | NAVIGATION **2**

41 **Bennachie**
9km | TRAIL | NAVIGATION **1**

42 **Loch Affric**
18km | TRAIL | NAVIGATION **3**

43 **Ben Hope**
9km | TRAIL | NAVIGATION **4**

44 **Fair Isle**
16km | TRAIL | NAVIGATION **3**

45 **Meall a' Bhuachaille Ridge**
16km | TRAIL | NAVIGATION **3**

46 **Merrick Circular**
14km | FELL | NAVIGATION **3**

47 **Devil's Beef Tub**
23km | TRAIL | NAVIGATION **1**

48 **Barra**
23km | FELL | NAVIGATION **1**

49 **Foinaven Circuit**
19km | MOUNTAIN | NAVIGATION **4**

50 **Kinlochewe to Dundonnell**
35km | FELL | NAVIGATION **3**

51 **Paps of Jura**
16km | MOUNTAIN | NAVIGATION **4**

52 **Loch Muick and Capel Mounth**
26km | FELL | NAVIGATION **4**

53 **Ring of Steall**
17km | MOUNTAIN | NAVIGATION **4**

54 **Lairig Ghru**
31km | FELL | NAVIGATION **2**

55 **Suilven**
20km | MOUNTAIN | NAVIGATION **4**

56 **White Mounth Munros**
29km | FELL | NAVIGATION **3**

57 **Rum Cuillin**
22km | MOUNTAIN | NAVIGATION **4**

58 **Ochil 2000s**
34km | FELL | NAVIGATION **2**

59 **Pentland Skyline**
28km | TRAIL | NAVIGATION **3**

60 **The Arran Corbetts**
25km | MOUNTAIN | NAVIGATION **4**

61 **South Glen Shiel Ridge**
27km | FELL | NAVIGATION **4**

62 **Trotternish Ridge**
30km | FELL | NAVIGATION **4**

63 **St John's Town of Dalry to Sanquhar**
42km | TRAIL | NAVIGATION **1**

64 **Lochaber Traverse**
30km | MOUNTAIN | NAVIGATION **4**

65 **Knoydart Traverse**
46km | FELL | NAVIGATION **3**

66 **Cairngorm 4000s**
40km | MOUNTAIN | NAVIGATION **4**

67 **Tyndrum to Fort William**
67km | TRAIL | NAVIGATION **1**

68 **Loch Mullardoch Round**
57km | FELL | NAVIGATION **4**

69 **Charlie Ramsay Round**
94km | MOUNTAIN | NAVIGATION **4**

70 **Munro Round**
c. 1,400km | FELL | NAVIGATION **4**

35
MUGDOCK COUNTRY PARK

5km | **TRAIL** | **NAVIGATION** 1 fully waymarked
CENTRAL AND SOUTHERN SCOTLAND

A great introductory-level trail run near
the city of Glasgow with views of the
Campsie Fells.

DISTANCE **5km**   ASCENT **80m**   TIME **0:20–0:40 hours**
START/FINISH **Mugdock Country Park visitor centre**   GRID REF **NS 546 779**
GPS **55.9723, -4.3308**   PUBLIC TRANSPORT **Buses and trains run from Glasgow to Milngavie, then it's a 20-minute walk to the park**
PARKING **Mugdock Country Park car park (free)**

© SHUTTERSTOCK/MOUNTAINTREKS

Mugdock Country Park comprises a huge 270
hectares of woodland, moorland and heathland just
13 kilometres from the city centre, making it one of
Glasgow's most treasured green spaces. It is littered
with historical marvels such as castles, mansions,
gallows, walled gardens and even an anti-aircraft gun
site from World War II.

The first kilometre of the route is almost entirely
downhill to Mugdock Loch. Pleasant running around
the lochshore leads to a gradual climb up to the ruins of
Mugdock Castle and on to the gun site. Don't forget to
take in the views across Glasgow on your left and the
Campsie Fells to your right. After the gun site the route
loops through a car park and descends on to a trail near
the loch. Dig deep for one final climb before arriving
back at the visitor centre for tea and cake.

OTHER OPTIONS Extend this route by starting from Milngavie town centre and running to the park via the West
Highland Way. Or grab a free map from the visitor
centre and extend your route via the park's many trails.
Longer challenges could incorporate Dumgoyne and
the Strathblane Hills, or trails around Burncrooks and
Kilmannan reservoirs via the John Muir Way.

RACE The Milngavie Trail Race takes place in June each
year, *www.runabc.co.uk/milngavie-trail-race* There are
sometimes CaniCross events here too if you want to
run with your dog, *www.canicross.org.uk*

WHAT NEXT? In Scotland, you can find similar trails at
Rothiemurchus in the Cairngorms, or Glentress in the
Borders. Elsewhere in Great Britain, try Kielder Forest
in Northumberland; Whinlatter Forest in the Lake
District; Haldon Forest Park in Devon; Salcey Forest
in Northamptonshire; Dalby Forest on the North York
Moors; Cannock Chase in Staffordshire; or Coed-y-
Brenin in Eryri (see page 144).

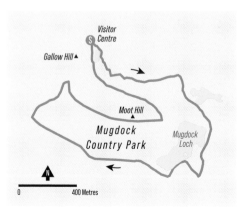

36
LOCH AN EILEIN

5km | TRAIL | NAVIGATION 2 partial waymarking
EASTERN SCOTLAND AND THE CAIRNGORMS

DISTANCE **5km**   ASCENT **70m**   TIME **0:25–0:45 hours**
START/FINISH **Loch an Eilein car park**   GRID REF **NH 897 085**
GPS **57.1540, -3.8249**   PUBLIC TRANSPORT **Local buses stop
in Inverdruie, which is about 1.5 kilometres from the start,
www.travelinescotland.com**   PARKING **Loch an Eilein car park
(parking charges apply)**

A picturesque trail around a much-loved
Scottish loch with a ruined castle on an island.

Scottish lochs don't get more photogenic and accessible than Loch an Eilein (the loch of the island), with
its ancient Scots pines and its ruined castle out on the
water.
    The route circumnavigates the loch on some of
the best low-level trails in Scotland. The trail weaves
through beautiful pinewoods which are a haven for
wildlife, and it is no surprise that this picturesque place
was once voted Britain's favourite picnic spot.

The island castle dates back to the late 14th century
when it was built as a refuge from thieves – have a look
in the visitor centre for the full story of its turbulent past.
According to legend, a zigzag underwater causeway
once linked the island to the shore, though no evidence
has ever been found of this.

OTHER OPTIONS
To extend the route, take the trail around Loch
Gamhna from the south-west tip of Loch an Eilein –
this can be boggy. These trails also link to the Lairig
Ghru and Gleann Eanaich.

WHAT NEXT?
Similar routes include the trails at nearby Rothiemurchus,
Loch Morlich or Loch Garten. Other great places for
waterside running include Llyn Crafnant or Llyn Idwal
in Eryri (see page 120); Easedale Tarn in the Lake
District; the Birks of Aberfeldy near Pitlochry; or the
Teign Gorge circuit in Devon for a look at Castle Drogo.

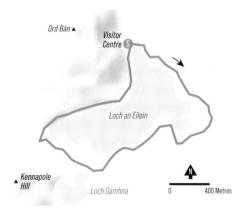

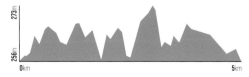

BOTH PHOTOS © KEN DOUGLAS

37

CRATHES CASTLE PARKRUN

5km | **TRAIL** | **NAVIGATION** 1 fully waymarked
EASTERN SCOTLAND AND THE CAIRNGORMS

A beautiful short trail run, winding through ancient woodland around Crathes Castle near Banchory.

DISTANCE **5km** ASCENT **80m** TIME **0:20–0:40 hours**
RECORDS **(F) 0:18.42; (M) 0:16.17** START/FINISH **Crathes Castle**
GRID REF **NO 734 968** GPS **57.0614, -2.4402** PUBLIC TRANSPORT **Regular buses run to the castle entrance on the A93 from Banchory and Aberdeen, www.travelinescotland.com** PARKING **Crathes Castle car park (parking charges apply)**

Crathes Castle was built in the 16th century and is home to some beautiful grounds and a historic walled garden. The site hosts the Crathes Castle parkrun every Saturday which is marked and marshalled. The route is only marked on parkrun days, though there are a number of waymarked trails through the grounds.

The parkrun forms a rough figure-of-eight, with the larger loop at the start. From the castle, the larger loop follows a tarmac path downhill towards the West Lodge but turns right uphill through the trees just before it. At the top of the hill, it swings right then heads downhill across the main tarmac path, turning left into the woodland. From here it proceeds beside the main drive, diverts right on to the smaller loop though the woods, then returns beside the main drive.

The finish sends runners uphill to re-join the tarmac path adjacent to the walled gardens. This steeper section takes runners back to the castle to finish. The views are excellent throughout but beware the hilly finish.

If you visit the castle, keep your eyes peeled, as it is said to be haunted by the Green Lady.

OTHER OPTIONS There are several waymarked trails suitable for running which explore the beautiful grounds – maps are all available from the estate.

RACE For further information or to register for the parkrun here, visit *www.parkrun.org.uk/crathescastle*

WHAT NEXT? For a tough course check out Drumchapel parkrun in Glasgow. Other popular courses in Scotland are Vogrie in Midlothian; Mount Stuart on the Isle of Bute; and Faskally Forest in Perthshire. For great views try Lews Castle parkrun in the Outer Hebrides. Elsewhere in Great Britain, Whinlatter Forest and Dolgeallau parkruns (see pages 2 and 120) are worth travelling for.

38
LOCH CORUISK

7km | **TRAIL** | **NAVIGATION** 3 *no waymarking*
SKYE

A lap of Scotland's most scenic loch, nestled within the dramatic Black Cuillin.

DISTANCE **7km** ASCENT **60m** TIME **0:50–1:30 hours**
START/FINISH **Landing stage next to Loch na Cuilce** GRID REF **NG 486 195** GPS **57.1976, -6.1630** ACCESS **By boat from Elgol (www. mistyisleboattrips.co.uk, www.bellajane.co.uk) or via the coastal path from Elgol (see below)** PARKING **Roadside parking is available in Elgol** MORE INFO **Loch Coruisk is sheltered by the eastern foothills of the infamous Cuillin Ridge**

The appeal of this challenge lies in the incredible majesty of the surroundings and the remote location of the freshwater loch, which is most easily accessed by boat. The unique adventure and spectacular setting outweighs the quality of the trail itself, which can be wet and boggy in places. The boat from Elgol drops you into the heart of the Cuillin (often after a spot of seal-watching).

The trail crosses the Scavaig River (said to be Britain's shortest river at a few hundred metres long) and follows the lochshore, avoiding the higher trail which climbs over the pass towards Glen Sligachan. You'll weave through boggy and rocky sections, as well as some giant grey boulders, to reach the head of the loch, where you can enjoy fantastic views of the mountains. The trail along the opposite shore has boggy sections which can be negotiated by linking protruding slabs and leads pleasantly back to the Scavaig River.

OTHER OPTIONS The easiest way back from Loch Coruisk is by boat. To extend the adventure, run out to Elgol via the trail leading south-east from the outflow of the loch towards Loch nan Leachd. The route leads via 'the bad step' (easily negotiated by confident scramblers) and past Camasunary bothy before hugging the coastline to reach the village of Elgol.

WHAT NEXT? For similar short but rugged trails on Skye you could try nearby Coire Làgan or a circuit of the Quiraing. Alternatively visit Corrie Fee in the Cairngorms; run a loop around Stac Pollaidh in Assynt;

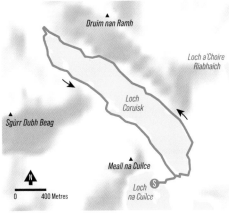

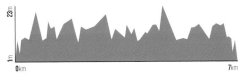

or visit the island of Kerrera in Argyll and Bute. For something longer and slightly more runnable (but equally remote), try the trails around Loch Affric or Loch Ossian in Highland; or Loch Muick in the Cairngorms. Elsewhere in Great Britain, try Llyn Idwal in Eryri (see page 120); Cheddar Gorge in Somerset; Beachy Head and the Seven Sisters in East Sussex (see page 17); Ynys Gybi (Holy Island) (see page 150), the Lizard Point Loop in Cornwall; or the Jurassic Coast sections of the South West Coastal Path.

39
LOWER LARGO TO ELIE

11km | **TRAIL** | **NAVIGATION** 1 fully waymarked
CENTRAL AND SOUTHERN SCOTLAND

A run along a stunning section of the Fife Coastal Path to find dunes, sandy beaches and Scotland's secret via ferrata!

DISTANCE **11km**   ASCENT **130m**   TIME **0:45–1:30 hours**
START **Lower Largo**   FINISH **Elie**   GRID REF **NO 422 026/NT 496 997**
GPS **56.2124, -2.9334/56.1872, -2.8123**   PUBLIC TRANSPORT **Regular direct bus connection between Lower Largo and Elie, www. travelinescotland.com**   PARKING **Lower Largo car park (free)**

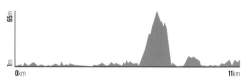

40
CONIC HILL

5km | **TRAIL** | **NAVIGATION** 2 partial waymarking
SOUTHERN HIGHLANDS

A short, sharp hill run on the Highland Boundary Fault, offering fantastic views over Loch Lomond.

DISTANCE **5km**   ASCENT **310m**   TIME **0:45–1:30 hours**
START/FINISH **Balmaha**   GRID REF **NS 421 909**   GPS **56.0847, -4.5391**
PUBLIC TRANSPORT **Good connections via bus (www.travelinescotland. com) and waterbus (high season only; www.cruiselochlomond.co.uk)**
PARKING **Balmaha car park (free)**

At 361 metres, Conic Hill is the highest point on the southern section of the West Highland Way and one of Scotland's most popular short hikes. On a clear day you can see Goatfell on the Isle of Arran (about 65 kilometres to the south-west)!

The trail is easy to follow, with man-made steps in places, passing through woodland and heading up pleasant open hillside on the eastern flank of the Conic

BOTH PHOTOS © CHRIS UPSON

Lower Largo was once the home of Alexander Selkirk, who is thought to have been the inspiration for Daniel Defoe's *Robinson Crusoe*. The route starts by crossing the beach, passing the remains of coastal defences from World War II. The sandy trail leads through the dunes and above Shell Bay, continuing along the coastal path and climbing above impressive basalt cliffs to reach Kincraig Point. Here you have two options: either continue on the coast path past more defence bunkers to reach communication masts and the top of Kincraig Hill (a natural viewpoint over the beaches to the east and west), or join the Elie Chain Walk.

A trail leads steeply down to some precarious steps cut into the rock (accessible only at low tide) to the Elie Chain Walk. (Take great care here and check the tide times for Anstruther Easter in advance. Start the chain walk no less than two hours before high tide.) This entertaining sting in the tail requires some scrambling ability to negotiate the rocky footholds and chains. After the chain walk, continue alongside a golf course to finish the route in Elie.

OTHER OPTIONS Extend this route by continuing on past the ruins of a clifftop castle to St Monans. You might consider additional sections of the Fife Coastal Path. Why not try the full coastal path as a relay! In 2013, a team of six runners from Carnethy Hill Running Club set a mark of 15 hours and 10 minutes for running the full Fife Coastal Path as a relay.

ULTRA ROUTE The Fife Coastal Path is a waymarked long-distance trail linking the Forth and Tay estuaries. It passes through the varied landscapes of Fife, linking sandy beaches, historical sites and picturesque fishing villages. The FKT belongs to (M) James Stewart who ran the 183-kilometre trail in 19:32.08 minutes in 2021.

WHAT NEXT? Similar Scottish routes include sections of the Moray Coast Trail or the Kintyre Way. Elsewhere in Great Britain, the Isle of Anglesey Coastal Path, Norfolk Coast Path or the South West Coast Path offer up equally fantastic coastline trails.

Hill ridge. After the col, you leave the West Highland Way and take a steep trail to the summit of Conic Hill, before descending back via the West Highland Way. The beautiful string of islands across Loch Lomond delineates the line of the Highland Boundary Fault, which Conic Hill is also on.

If you have time, you may wish to clamber up to the viewpoint of Craigie Fort on your way back along the shore of Loch Lomond.

OTHER OPTIONS This route can be shortened by returning back to Balmaha the same way as you came; via the West Highland Way from Bealach Ard.

RACE The West Highland Way Race covers the full length of the trail, including Conic Hill, *www.westhighlandwayrace.org*

WHAT NEXT? For similar small hills in Scotland try Meall a' Bhuachaille in the Cairngorms (see page 68); Stac Pollaidh in Assynt; the Cobbler in Loch Lomond and the Trossachs; or Bennachie in Aberdeenshire (see page 62). Elsewhere in Great Britain, Cat Bells (see page 4) or Silver How the Lake District; Roseberry Topping in North Yorkshire; Cleeve Hill in the Cotswolds; Moel Eilio in Eryri (see page 132); or Sugar Loaf in the Black Mountains (see page 128) are well worth a look.

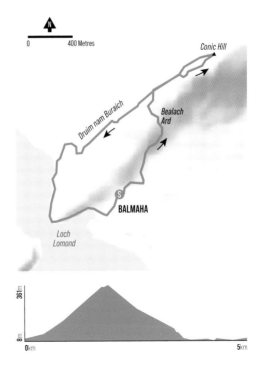

41

BENNACHIE

9km | **TRAIL** | **NAVIGATION** 1 fully waymarked
EASTERN SCOTLAND AND THE CAIRNGORMS

A lovely runnable trail linking the main peaks of Bennachie with views over Aberdeenshire.

| DISTANCE **9km** ASCENT **400m** TIME **1:10–2:20 hours**
| START/FINISH **Back o' Bennachie, off the B9002** GRID REF **NJ 661 247**
| GPS **57.3117, -2.5627** PUBLIC TRANSPORT **No practical options**
| PARKING **Back o' Bennachie car park (parking charges apply)**

North East Scotland's most prominent landmark, Bennachie, is a runners' playground and is also littered with interesting archaeological sights – a Pictish hillfort, recumbent stone circles and even old aeroplane wreckage near Oxen Craig. For information on the history of the area visit *www.bailiesofbennachie.co.uk*

This route takes in the two highest peaks in the area – Oxen Craig and Mither Tap. The well-signposted Mither Tap Quarry Trail leads out of the forest, passing an old quarry at Little Oxen Craig (the source of stone for house building in the nearby villages until its access road was washed away in the late 19th century), and up granite slabs on to Oxen Craig (529 metres). From this fantastic viewpoint, you can see Mither Tap, your next destination, which is topped by a hillfort with massive walls.

From Mither Tap, the trail branches out to the smaller 480-metre Craigshannoch before rejoining the outward route at Little Oxen Craig.

OTHER OPTIONS To lengthen, follow the Bennachie Hill Race route (see below). To shorten, take any left turn between Oxen Craig and Mither Tap to rejoin the return route earlier. There are other short waymarked trails in the forest – *www.forestryandland.gov.scot/visit/back-o-bennachie*

RACE Bennachie Hill Race (organised by Garioch RoadRunners) follows a longer, 13-kilometre route and is part of the Aberdeenshire Hill Races series. Course records belong to (F) Clare Whitehead at 1:01.25 in 2002 and (M) Rob Sinclair at 0:51.58 in 2022.

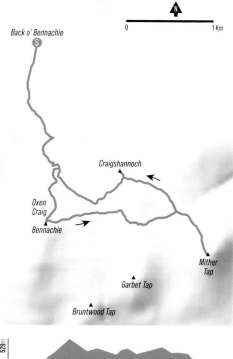

WHAT NEXT? For another ancient hillfort race route in Aberdeenshire try Dunnydeer. Other similar hills in the Aberdeenshire area include Clachnaben, Cairn William and Morven. For something longer try a circuit of the Correen Hills in Aberdeenshire or Mount Keen in the Cairngorms for a runnable Munro. Other notable small hill challenges in the UK include Brown Willy in Cornwall (see page 4); Roseberry Topping in North Yorkshire; Pendle Hill in Lancashire (see page 6); Chrome Hill or Stanage Edge in the Peak District; or Castle Crag in the Lake District.

42
LOCH AFFRIC

18km | **TRAIL** | **NAVIGATION 3** no waymarking
WESTERN HIGHLANDS

A remote lochside trail in the picturesque
Glen Affric National Nature Reserve.

DISTANCE **18km** ASCENT **300m** TIME **1:45–2:45 hours**
START/FINISH **River Affric car park, Glen Affric** GRID REF **NH 201 233**
GPS **57.2649, -4.9847** PUBLIC TRANSPORT **No practical options**
PARKING **River Affric car park (parking charges apply)**

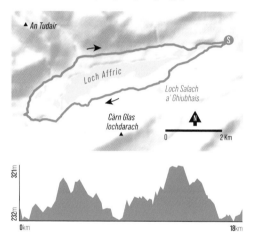

Glen Affric is often described as the most beautiful
glen in Scotland. It stretches around 50 kilometres,
from Cannich in Strathglass in the east to Kintail in
the west and is home to one of the largest ancient
Caledonian pine forests remaining in Scotland today.

The route starts at the eastern end of Loch Affric,
heading west along the southern shore of the loch along
part of the Affric Kintail Way. The trail goes through
beautiful woodland with views of Affric Lodge across
the water. At the far end of the loch, don't miss the right
turn on to the lower rocky track past some abandoned
buildings and Athnamulloch bothy. The trail ascends
past Strawberry Cottage, then you take a narrow
trail towards Loch Coulavie, which provides some
interesting undulating running back past Affric Lodge.

OTHER OPTIONS The route can be extended with an out-
and-back run to Glen Affric Youth Hostel at Alltbeithe
or the Camban bothy beyond. Alternatively, the route
can be started further east, at Dog Falls car park at the
eastern end of the stunning Loch Beinn a' Mheadhoin.
The Affric Kintail Way crosses the River Affric and
road here.

WHAT NEXT? For similar trails try Loch Muick in the
Cairngorms; Loch Ossian in Highland; or Loch Coruisk
on the Isle of Skye (see page 59). For remoteness, try
some sections of the Cape Wrath Trail. Elsewhere in
Great Britain, you might consider routes through the
quiet Berwyn Hills (see page 134); the Moelwynion
area of Eryri; the Howgills or the Cheviots.

43

BEN HOPE

9km | **TRAIL** | **NAVIGATION** **4** difficult self-navigation
or complex terrain
NORTH WEST HIGHLANDS

Run the most northerly Munro in Scotland!
This tough climb is rewarded by views to the
Orkney Islands and Faroe Islands on a clear day.

DISTANCE **9km**   ASCENT **950m**   TIME **1:40–2:40 hours**
START/FINISH **Muiseal, Strath More**   GRID REF **NC 461 477**
GPS **58.3905, -4.6344**   PUBLIC TRANSPORT **No practical options**
PARKING **Small car park at Muiseal (free)**

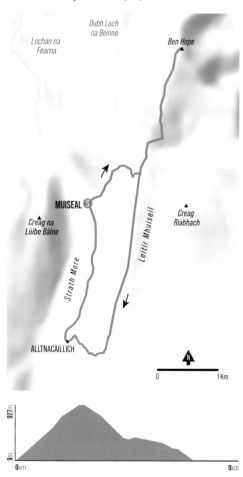

Ben Hope summit is famed for its breathtaking views
over a vast desolate wilderness dotted with lochans
and isolated peaks, while the sea beyond stretches
away towards the Arctic – consider saving this
challenge for a clear day.

The popular trail starts with a large sign marking
the *Way Up Ben Hope*. Embrace the stiff initial climb,
which is rocky in places, gaining height alongside the
Allt a' Mhuiseil. Higher up, you cross the river before
the trail steepens once more, weaving through craggy
ground to emerge above the escarpment. This grassy
shelf leads up to the broad south ridge of Ben Hope, but
the summit is not as close as it might appear! Before the
top is reached the trail makes a deviation to the right to
ascend through yet another steeper section. Above this,
the trail is more obvious and continues to climb up a
grassy slope to a false summit. A further push delivers
the summit trig point and its splendid panorama.

On the way down continue south along the escarpment of Leitir Mhuiseil to the waterfall above Alltna-
caillich, then follow the southern bank of the Allt na
Caillich down to the road. Warm down with a short
jog along the road heading north back to the car park.

OTHER OPTIONS A basic out-and-back up Ben Hope is a
shorter option (plus it removes the jaunt along the
road), but cuts short a lovely descent and misses the
fine waterfall. To add to the challenge, Ben Hope can
also be reached by a tougher route, starting from the
southern tip of Loch Hope, via some very exposed
scrambling up the northern ridge.

WHAT NEXT? For alternative hills in the area, Ben Loyal
and Ben Stack give great running in an equally remote
and impressive setting. Elsewhere in Scotland try
Goatfell on the Isle of Arran; Buachaille Etive Mòr
in Glen Coe; or The Devils' Point (Càirn Toul) in the
Cairngorms for a similar top viewpoint experience.
Across Great Britain, you could add Tryfan in Eryri;
Great Gable in the Lake District; or Pen y Fan in the
Brecon Beacons (see page 129) to you your tick list
of iconic mountains.

44
FAIR ISLE

16km | **TRAIL** | **NAVIGATION** **3** no waymarking
SHETLAND ISLANDS

Explore the grassy clifftops and impressive coastal scenery of one of the most remote inhabited islands in Great Britain.

DISTANCE **16km** ASCENT **350m** TIME **2–3 hours** START/FINISH **Fair Isle airstrip** GRID REF **HZ 211 720** GPS **59.5333, -1.6287** PUBLIC TRANSPORT **Connections from Shetland Mainland via sea or by air**

Fair Isle is isolated, even by Shetland standards! But despite being tiny (less than 5 kilometres long) it offers an excellent wee adventure.

The route heads up to the trig point of Ward Hill which, at 217 metres, is the highest point of the island and qualifies as a Marilyn. It then follows the western coastline of the island over Burrashield and Hoini, passing deep geos (narrow clefts formed by erosion in coastal cliffs). Several headlands must be negotiated before you reach Malcolm's Head, which is marked by an old coastguard lookout. The trail continues around the coastline, visiting a lighthouse and giving views of The Burrian (a rocky outcrop out to sea). Be sure to look out for puffins as you climb the headland overlooking Sheep Rock.

OTHER OPTIONS Shorten by leaving out Ward Hill and taking the road directly to Stonybreck, before heading to the western coastline much further south at Reeva (just north of Malcolm's Head). The distance can also be extended by exploring the more rugged northern end of the island, including Skroo Lighthouse.

WHAT NEXT? Shetland boasts around 2,700 kilometres of spectacular coastline and many of the 100 islands have established circular trails. Details of these can be found at *www.shetland.org/visit/do/outdoors/walk* Good examples include the St Ninian's Isle Circular (6 kilometres) or the longer Papa Stour Circular (17 kilometres).

© PAUL WEBSTER

Ward Hill

Fair Isle

Goorn

Fogli Stack

Sheep Rock

Malcolm's Head

Meo Ness

0   1 Km

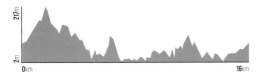

217m

2m

0km   16km

45

MEALL A' BHUACHAILLE RIDGE

16km | TRAIL | NAVIGATION 3 no waymarking
EASTERN SCOTLAND AND THE CAIRNGORMS

An accessible, classic hill run with Cairn Gorm as a backdrop.

DISTANCE **16km** ASCENT **630m** TIME **2:15–3:15 hours**
START/FINISH **Glenmore Visitor Centre** GRID REF **NH 978 098**
GPS **57.1676, -3.6916** PUBLIC TRANSPORT **Nearest train station is Aviemore. Regular buses run between Aviemore and the Cairngorm Mountain resort passing the visitor centre** PARKING **Glenmore Visitor Centre car park (parking charges apply). There are several other car parks nearby, but all are busy in high season**

The Meall a' Bhuachaille ridgeline is home to a classic Scottish hill race but is also a popular running challenge in its own right. It's an ideal choice for beginners and a great poor weather option.

The route heads through ancient pine and birch forest, passing close to An Lochan Uaine (the so-called 'green lochan'), and reaching Ryvoan bothy at the head of the Ryvoan Pass. Behind the bothy, a well-maintained hill path climbs up Meall a' Bhuachaille, then its neighbour Creagan Gorm, from where a marvellous undulating ridge leads to Craiggowrie. The lower section of the trail back through the forest is boggy and indistinct until you reach the main forest track.

OTHER OPTIONS To shorten the route, descend south from the first col (at 624 metres) after Meall a' Bhuachaille summit, and take the trail into the forest via Coire Chondlaich. This leads directly back towards Glenmore. A slightly longer alternative from Glenmore is the hill trail to Bynack More.

RACE The Meall a' Bhuachaille race is a classic of the Scottish hill running calendar. The route taken is similar, ticking off all the summits along the ridgeline, but it ascends Coire Chondlaich and climbs Meall a' Bhuachaille as an out-and-back from the col, rather than going via Ryvoan bothy. The race starts and finishes at Badaguish.

WHAT NEXT? For similar accessible hills in Scotland try the Cobbler or Ben A'an in Loch Lomond and the Trossachs; Tinto in South Lanarkshire; Scald Law in the Pentland Hills; Cort-ma Law in the Campsie Fells; Ben Vrackie in Perth and Kinross; or the Whangie in the Kilpatrick Hills. Elsewhere in Great Britain you could try Silver How the Lake District; High Cup Nick in the North Pennines (page 20); Mam Tor in the Peak District (page 24); or Ingleborough in the Yorkshire Dales (page 35).

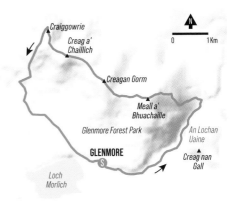

Craiggowrie

Creag a' Chaillich

Creagan Gorm

Meall a' Bhuachaille

Glenmore Forest Park

An Lochan Uaine

GLENMORE

Creag nan Gall

Loch Morlich

N

0   1Km

46
MERRICK CIRCULAR

14km | FELL | NAVIGATION 3 no waymarking
CENTRAL AND SOUTHERN SCOTLAND

Superb grassy hill running over Merrick, the
Southern Uplands' most popular summit and
highpoint of the evocatively named Range of
the Awful Hand.

DISTANCE **14km**   ASCENT **840m**   TIME **2:15–3:15 hours**   START/FINISH
Upper Bruce's Stone car park, Loch Trool   GRID REF **NX 415 804**
GPS **55.0930, -4.4840**   PUBLIC TRANSPORT **No practical options**
PARKING **Upper Bruce's Stone car park (free)**

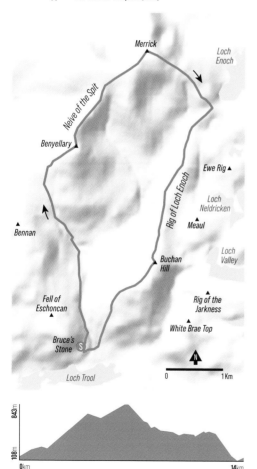

Merrick is the highest mountain in the Southern
Uplands and overlooks picturesque Loch Trool in
Galloway Forest Park.

A good trail weaves up beside the waterfalls of
the Buchan Burn and down to Culsharg bothy. From
Benyellary, you continue via the impressive Neive of
the Spit ridge and up the broad flank of Merrick to
the trig point at 843 metres. The Ring of Fire route
(see right) continues north from here, but this route
veers south-east down the rough ground of Redstone
Rig. There follows fantastic panoramic rough running
along the undulating Rig of Loch Enoch to Buchan
Hill, with views of several lochs and the evocatively
named Dungeon Hill, Craignaw, the Point of the Snibe
and the Rig of the Jarkness. The ominous-sounding
Murder Hole on the OS map was relocated here from
Glen Trool by the novelist S.R. Crockett for literary
convenience, however. The descent gully on the south-
west of the summit of Buchan Hill is flanked by craggy
spurs and requires some care to negotiate safely.

OTHER OPTIONS Returning the same way from the summit of Benyellary or Merrick is less navigationally challenging, and a good way of shortening the route. To lengthen the adventure, link Merrick with Kirrie-reoch Hill, Tarfessock and Shalloch on Minnoch in a linear route from Loch Trool to the road south of Stinchar Bridge.

ULTRA ROUTE The full Ring of Fire is a 72-kilometre round with 4,000 metres of ascent over 30 summits in the Galloway Hills. The route links the Range of the Awful Hand, the Rhinns of Kells and the Minnigaff Hills. Remote and trackless, the round was created by hill walker Andy Priestman, but it was first completed by local crofter Glyn Jones who ran it under 24 hours in 1990. Jonny Muir set a new FKT for the round of 14 hours and 6 minutes in 2018, despite twisting an ankle en route and concluding that it was 'very hard'. At the time of writing there is no recorded FKT by a woman.

RACE The Merrick Hill Race (14 kilometres with 1,000 metres of ascent) takes place each September.

WHAT NEXT? Other similar hill running circuits in Scotland include the Rois-Bheinn round in Moidart; the Glenfinnan Munros; Cairn Gorm and the Northern Corries; or the Foinaven Circuit in the North West Highlands (see page 74). Elsewhere try the Kentmere Skyline, the Old Man of Coniston, or the Buttermere and Hay Stacks circular in the Lake District; Drygarn Fawr or Pen Pumlumon Fawr in the Cambrian Mountains (see pages 130 and 126); or Cnicht from Llyn Edno in Eryri.

For alternatives to the Ring of Fire ultra route try the Meirionnydd Round (see page 124); the Broxap Round in the Western Highlands (see page 98); or the Etive Munros Round or the shorter Glen Coe Corbetts Round in Glen Coe.

47

DEVIL'S BEEF TUB

23km | TRAIL | NAVIGATION 1 fully waymarked
CENTRAL AND SOUTHERN SCOTLAND

Circumnavigate the dramatic hollow of the
Devil's Beef Tub and complete the northern
section of the Annandale Way.

> DISTANCE **23km**   ASCENT **480m**   TIME **2:30-3:30 hours**   START/FINISH
> **Station Park, Moffat**   GRID REF **NT 084 049**   GPS **55.3295, -3.4453**
> PUBLIC TRANSPORT **Moffat has good bus links; Station Park is a short
> walk from the centre of Moffat**   PARKING **Moffat public car park (free)**

Source-to-sea routes form the basis of many
running challenges – and a great many more still lie
undiscovered! The Annandale Way is one of the most
recent of these; it was established in 2009 and is now
recognised as one of Scotland's Great Trails.

From Moffat, the route heads up Annandale then
climbs over Eric Stane, where impressive views over
the deep bowl of the Devil's Beef Tub open up – the
highlight of the route. This 150-metre-deep hollow was
used by the Border Reivers of the Johnstone clan (who
were called 'devils' by their enemies) to hide stolen
cattle; its shape is also thought to resemble the shape
of a meat-preserving tub. In 1685, a fleeing Covenanter
vainly attempted to escape the dragoons by running up
the steep side of the Beef Tub.

The route loops round via Annanhead Hill, where
the River Annan rises, and Peat Knowe, staying north
of the summit of Great Hill, and following Chalk Rig
Edge to Annandale Head, the most northerly point on
the Annandale Way. Head south beside Tweedhope
Burn then follow the River Annan as it wends its way
back to Moffat.

OTHER OPTIONS Extend the route by adding neighbouring
hills, such as Hart Fell – descending to Moffat via
Swatte Fell and Gallow Hill. Alternatively consider
additional sections of the Annandale Way; the next
logical stretch runs from Moffat to St Ann's. Note that
the Annandale Way intersects the Southern Upland
Way just outside Beattock near Moffat.

ULTRA ROUTE The Annandale Way follows the River
Annan from source to sea. It runs from Moffat (with a
loop north to Annandale Head) to Newbie Barns near

Annan on the Solway Firth. It is 90 kilometres long
with 1,150 metres of ascent; waymarking is generally
good. The FKTs (supported) are (M) Kevin Plummer
with 11 hours and 11 minutes in 2021 and (F) Elysha
Ramage with 12 hours and 47 minutes in 2022.
The fastest self-supported time belongs to (M) Rob
Mansbridge with 11 hours and 45 minutes in 2021.

WHAT NEXT? For similar trail and fell running routes in
the Southern Uplands try the Merrick Circular (see
page 70), the Culter Fell Circuit, the Durisdeer Hill
Race route or the Yetholm Hill Race route. Elsewhere
in the UK try the Cat Bells, Maiden Moor and High
Spy Circular in the Lake District; the Malvern Hills
(see page 16); or Moel Eilio in Eryri (see page 132).

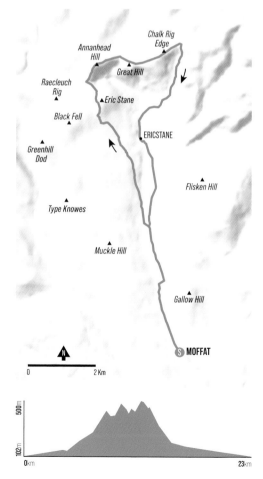

48

BARRA

23km | FELL | NAVIGATION 1 fully waymarked
OUTER HEBRIDES

© SHUTTERSTOCK/ABLANDIN

Run the length of Barra, from ferry slipway to ferry slipway, exploring a scenic section of the Hebridean Way.

The isles of Barra and Vatersay are the most southerly inhabited islands in the Outer Hebrides and the most westerly in Great Britain, boasting fabulous large white beaches popular for water sports.

Starting at Àird Mhòr in the north of the island, the route follows the Hebridean Way across pathless heather and moorland, with helpful posts to keep you on track. The way passes between Dùn Bharpa and Grianan, then veers west to the coast at Bàgh Halaman. Yellow marker posts lead to the remains of Dùn Bàn, an Iron Age hillfort, then head back inland over the flank of Beinn Tangabhal, with views across Vatersay and the uninhabited Bishop's Isles. This section is often pathless and the waymarking is not very obvious. Beside the Allt Chrisal burn you can see the remains of a Neolithic roundhouse before you reach the road near the causeway leading to Vatersay.

From hear you leave the Hebridean Way and walk along roads to the ferry terminal at Castlebay.

OTHER OPTIONS For a longer challenge, the route could be completed south to north, taking in Vatersay first. Catch the ferry at Àird Mhòr to Eriskay and keep going north to visit the next islands in the chain.

Another longer alternative is to run south to north and then return to Castlebay, via the A888 around the eastern side of the island. This was part of the official 'Barrathon' route, a now-defunct road race round the isle.

ULTRA ROUTE The Hebridean Way is a unique 251-kilometre trail that stretches the length of the Outer Hebrides from Vatersay in the south to Stornoway in the north. It covers ten islands, six causeways and two ferry crossings, with a mix of hill and coastal scenery.

RACE The Hebridean Way forms the basis of The Isles Ultra by Rat Race. For more information or to enter, visit *www.ratrace.com/the-isles-ultra*

DISTANCE **23km** ASCENT **580m** TIME **2:45–3:45 hours** START **Àird Mhòr slipway** FINISH **Castlebay slipway** GRID REF **NF 720 038/ NL 665 983** GPS **57.0084, -7.4053/56.9552, -7.4888** PUBLIC TRANSPORT **Catch the ferry from Oban to Castlebay, in the south of Barra. From here catch a bus to Àird Mhòr to start the route. You can also fly to Barra from Glasgow and land on the beach!** MORE INFO **www.visitouterhebrides.co.uk/hebrideanway**

WHAT NEXT? For more adventures on the West Coast of Scotland take a look at the Kintyre Way, West Island Way or the Arran Coastal Way. The round of Fair Isle (see page 67) is an equally unique and remote Scottish experience. Elsewhere in Great Britain, try the fabulous coastal trails of the Isle of Anglesey Coastal Path, Pembrokeshire Coast Path or the South West Coast Path.

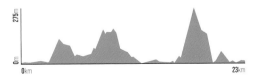

49

FOINAVEN CIRCUIT

19km | **MOUNTAIN** | **NAVIGATION 4** difficult self-
navigation or complex terrain
NORTH WEST HIGHLANDS

A circular route over the magnificent Foinaven
ridge, Great Britain's most northerly ridge
running adventure and one of the most
spectacular mountains in Sutherland.

| DISTANCE **19km**   ASCENT **920m**   TIME **2:50–3:50 hours**   START/FINISH
| **Small quarry on the A838, north of Gualin House**   GRID REF **NC 308 567**
| GPS **58.4657, -4.9019**   PUBLIC TRANSPORT **No practical options**
| PARKING **Lay-by parking (free) – please park considerately**

© FINLAY WILD

A memorable experience for the true enthusiast,
Foinaven rises majestically from the flat lands of
Sutherland, a stunning and complex mountain with
many dramatic ridges, coires and spurs. Once thought
to be a Munro, it was later reclassified as a Corbett,
missing the mark for Munro status by just 12 feet.

The challenge described here provides a logistically
simpler option than a full ridge traverse, while still
affording many of the same ridge-running opportunities and incredible views.

The route heads up Strath Dionard, then follows the
Allt Coire Dùail up into the coire, and on to Bealach
nan Càrn, from where you ascend a steep boulder field,

with the ridge becoming more defined as you gain height up to the summit of Ceann Garbh. Take a moment to soak up the impressive views from here, including Scotland's most northerly Munro, Ben Hope, and Glas-Choire Grànda lochan far below! Then continue up to the summit of Ganu Mòr, the highest point of the Foinaven ridge. Although the first cairn marks the highest point, the eastern cairn has the most impressive views – on a clear day you can see from the Orkney Islands to the Cuillins on the Isle of Skye. The descent avoids a series of crags, then crosses boggy moorland, passing between Lochan Sgeireach and Loch Tarbhaidh.

OTHER OPTIONS The shortest route to the summit is an out-and-back via the descent route described on the left. For a longer challenge, try the Foinaven-Arkle traverse (26 kilometres with 1,360 metres of ascent). This fabulous journey is a linear one, with the same start location but finishing on the A838, at the northern tip of Loch Stack.

WHAT NEXT? For other similar fell running challenges in the north of Scotland try Ben Loyal; Quinag; Suilven (see page 88) and Canisp; the Applecross Corbetts; or Ben More Assynt and Conival. Elsewhere in Great Britain, try running the Glyderau or Drum (see page 130) in Eryri or any of the great Lakeland horseshoes.

50
KINLOCHEWE TO DUNDONNELL

35km | FELL | NAVIGATION 3 no waymarking
WESTERN HIGHLANDS

A favourite stage of the Cape Wrath Trail, this route crosses the Great Wilderness and takes in an unbeatable mountain panorama deep in the Fisherfield Forest.

DISTANCE **35km** ASCENT **910m** TIME **3-5 hours** START **Kinlochewe**
FINISH **A832 near Dundonnell** GRID REF **NH 030 618/NH 114 850**
GPS **57.6039, -5.2984/57.8148, -5.1759** PUBLIC TRANSPORT **No practical options** PARKING **This through-route is logistically tricky but worth the effort. The start is an hour's drive from the finish by road, so requires a two-car shuttle, drop-off or hitch in between. There is a car park (free) at the start at Kinlochewe and lay-by parking at the finish at Dundonnell**

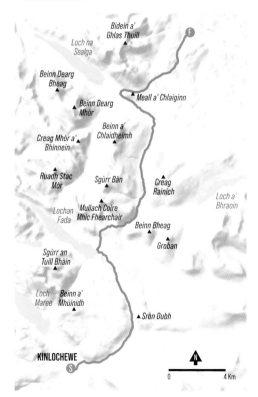

Although this route crosses the Great Wilderness – the Letterewe and Fisherfield forests – there are good paths and tracks for the most part, apart from the tough pathless section from Lochan Fada to Bealach na Croise. From here there is a path, and you follow the Abhainn Loch an Nid into the heart of the Fisherfield Forest. The trail deteriorates after Achneigie, but you will eventually arrive at the popular Shenavall bothy.

Take the trail behind the bothy that follows the Allt a' Chlaiginn. This boggy trod traverses the lower slopes of Sàil Liath, reaching a maximum height of 400 metres

near Lochan na Bràthan before dropping to join a much larger track above Loch Coire Chaorachain and finishing on the A832 near Dundonnell.

OTHER OPTIONS The Cape Wrath Trail naturally breaks into a number of recognised legs, which depend in the early stages on the route taken from Fort William to Morvich. They vary considerably in length and are all worth running in their own right and link to make excellent multi-day journeys. The stretch across Knoydart is another fantastic section.

Shenavall bothy is the best place from which to start a round of the Fisherfield Munros; an excellent round with unparalleled views throughout.

ULTRA ROUTE The full Cape Wrath Trail stretches for around 385 kilometres from Fort William to Cape Wrath, the most north-westerly point on the British mainland. It is unmarked throughout, with some route options along the way. It weaves through superb wild landscapes and between impressive mountain ranges for most of its length and is a committing undertaking, even for the most experienced. The FKT (Glenfinnan variant) belongs to (F) Rebecca Brennan with 5 days 5 hours and 36 minutes in 2022 and (M) Graham Connolly and Paul Giblin, with 3 days 23 hours and 45 minutes in 2021. Average time for the full trail is 7–10 days.

RACE The Cape Wrath Ultra is an eight-day stage race organised by Ourea Events. For more information or to enter, visit *www.capewrathultra.com*

WHAT NEXT? For a less remote but comparable undertaking you might consider the Skye Trail or sections of the Pennine Way, Offa's Dyke Path or the South West Coast Path.

© KERI WALLACE

51

PAPS OF JURA

16km | **MOUNTAIN** | **NAVIGATION 4** difficult self-navigation or complex terrain
INNER HEBRIDES

A rugged and unforgettable round over the three iconic summit of the Paps of Jura, surrounded on all sides by the sea.

DISTANCE **16km** ASCENT **1,450m** TIME **4–6 hours**
START/FINISH **Three Arch Bridge, A846** GRID REF **NR 544 720**
GPS **55.8787, -5.9268** PUBLIC TRANSPORT **Jura can be reached by a small car ferry via Islay or direct by ferry (high-speed RIB) from the mainland. Once on Jura, if you don't have a car a bike is a good way of getting around** PARKING **Lay-by on the north side of the Three Arch Bridge** MORE INFO **www.welcometojura.com**

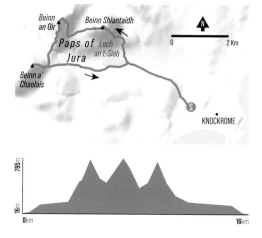

The route takes in the Paps of Jura – three distinctive, steep-sided quartzite hills on the southern part of the island of Jura. You'll first ascend the scree-covered eastern side of Beinn Shiantaidh – the 'Sacred Mountain' – before descending to a col, then following a vague trail past the remains of stone buildings with stunning views up to the rocky summit of Beinn an Oir – the 'Mountain of Gold – the highest of the three paps and the only Corbett. Beinn a' Chaolais – the 'Mountain of the Sound' – requires an out-and-back, before a boggy, pathless descent via Loch an t-Siob back to the bridge. You may spot deer grazing or an adder sunbathing along the way.

OTHER OPTIONS Any of the three Paps can be climbed on their own by starting at the Three Arch Bridge. It is possible to bail into Gleann an t-Siob' from any of the bealachs in this round and return to the start via Loch an t-Siob'. For a longer challenge try the full race route.

RACE The inaugural Isle of Jura Fell Race took place in 1973 and has since grown to become a popular classic of the fell running calendar – a sociable weekend of camping, fell running and island culture. Route finding can be difficult, particularly in poor visibility, as the route isn't obvious and passes through loose, technical and largely pathless terrain; good navigation skills are required.

The race route is 28 kilometres with 2,370 metres of ascent and includes not only the three Paps but also four smaller hills. Course records are held by (F) Jasmin Paris with 3 hours and 38 minutes in 2015 and (M) Finlay Wild with 2 hours and 58 minutes in 2022. For more information or to enter, visit *www.isleofjurafellrace.co.uk*

WHAT NEXT? For similar but less remote routes you could try rounds of the Glyderau in Eryri; the Langdale Pikes or the Old Man of Coniston in the Lake District; Rum Cuillin (see page 90); the Glamaig Hill Race route on Skye; the Kilnsey Crag Races route in the Yorkshire Dales; or the Foinaven Circuit in the North West Highlands (see page 74).

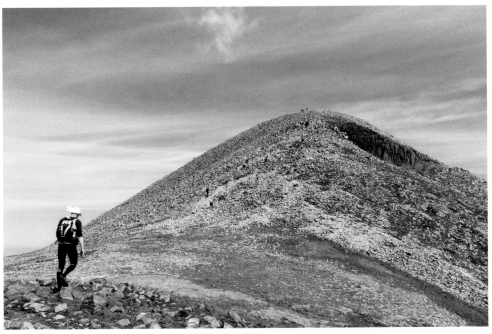

52

LOCH MUICK AND CAPEL MOUNTH

26km | **FELL** | **NAVIGATION** 4 difficult self-navigation
or complex terrain
EASTERN SCOTLAND AND THE CAIRNGORMS

Runnable loop over a grass-covered plateau
and past a remote loch on the quieter side
of the Cairngorms National Park.

DISTANCE **26km**   ASCENT **830m**   TIME **3:30–5:30 hours**
START/FINISH **Glendoll, Glen Clova**   GRID REF **NO 284 760**
GPS **56.8698, -3.1761**   PUBLIC TRANSPORT **No practical options**
PARKING **Glendoll car park (parking charges apply)**

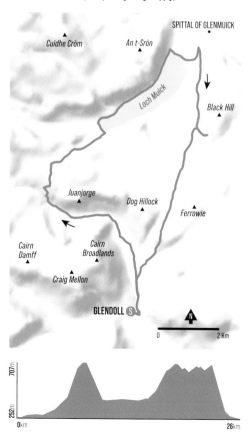

Beautiful Loch Muick is situated at the foot of
Lochnagar, one of Scotland's most impressive
mountains and part of the royal estate of Balmoral.
This challenge provides some fantastic trail and fell
running combined with a jaw-dropping panorama.

From Glendoll, the route heads upriver, following
the River South Esk to Bachnagairn, then turns more
steeply uphill to a junction of trails. Not far beyond
is Allan's Hut, a modern corrugated-iron stable for
stalkers' ponies that has replaced a tumbledown
wooden structure inside which walkers traditionally
pitched their tents … with the guy ropes passing
through the holes to be pegged outside! You then drop
steeply down to Loch Muick on the so-called 'Streak of
Lightning', which is also popular with mountain bikers.

Follow the trail round the attractive loch to the far end where the route joins Capel Road. This track, which has appeared on maps since the 14th century, was once a dangerous undertaking, as cairn memorials attest. It gives a steady 2-kilometre climb up on to the plateau and across the western side of Capel Mounth, before a descent with fantastic views on an excellent grassy trail beside the Capel Burn takes you back to the start.

OTHER OPTIONS For a shorter alternative, follow the original route until you reach Loch Muick. Turn right along the shoreline then loop back on to a higher track at Black Burn; this takes you along the top of the escarpment (heading south-west) until you reach Allan's Hut. Return via the outward route.

A simple loop of Loch Muick from the Spittal of Glenmuick car park is another good option.

Jock's Road in Glen Doll (west of the starting point) is a handy way to extend your run, providing access to the bigger hills south-west of Dubh Loch. Glen Doll is also a popular starting point for running the Munros Driesh and Mayar.

WHAT NEXT? For similar undulating routes try Cairn Gorm and Ben Macdui; or the Pentland Skyline (see page 94). Or for something bigger, try the the Lawers Range in Perth and Kinross; or the Creag Meagaidh Traverse in Highland. Elsewhere in Great Britain try the Brecon Beacons Horseshoe or any (perhaps all!) of the great horseshoes of the Lake District, or build up to the Edale Skyline (see page 24).

53
RING OF STEALL

17km | **MOUNTAIN** | **NAVIGATION** 4 difficult self-
navigation or complex terrain
WESTERN HIGHLANDS

A classic Scottish mountain round of four
majestic Munros with some airy ridge
scrambling in between.

DISTANCE **17km** ASCENT **1,350m** TIME **3–6 hours** RECORDS **(F) Jess
Acheson 3:18.47 in 2021; (M) Finlay Wild 1:57.34 in 2020**
START/FINISH **Lower Falls car park, Glen Nevis** GRID REF **NN 145 683**
GPS **56.7692, -5.0369** PUBLIC TRANSPORT **Regular bus service
between Fort William and Glen Nevis, www.travelinescotland.com**
PARKING **Lower Falls car park (parking charges apply)**

This challenge is a long-standing Scottish hillwalking
classic which has become popular with mountain
runners since the first Salomon Ring of Steall Skyrace
in 2016.

Its cirque of rocky peaks surrounds a single coire,
which holds a mighty waterfall called An Steall – hence
the name. The base of these falls can be accessed by
a quirky 'wire bridge', which is challenge enough for
some people.

The route follows the popular tourist trail through a
dramatic gorge, popping out in an idyllic flat glen with
An Steall at its heart, tumbling 120 metres down the
cliffs. Here you'll find the famous wire bridge which
consists of two handrails and a single wire for your feet.
It is also possible (if the river is not too high) to ford the
river just above the 'bridge'.

Boggy but improving ground leads to the long
steep climb to the summit of the first Munro, An
Gearanach. This is the start of a lofty ridge traverse
(grade 1 scramble) towards An Garbhanach. Continue
round the great coire, linking the second and third
Munros – Stob Coire a' Chàirn and Am Bodach – with
Sgùrr an Iubhair (which was briefly and inexplicably
promoted to Munro status between 1981 and 1997).
You must then traverse the Devil's Ridge, an exposed
and occasionally technical (grade 1) scramble to reach
the fourth and highest Munro on the route, Sgùrr a'
Mhàim (1,099 metres), with fantastic views over Ben
Nevis. Take care to descend north-west from here
avoiding steep ground until you pick up the trail back
to the glen.

OTHER OPTIONS It is possible to bail out to Kinlochleven
part way round – either from the col east of Stob Coire
a' Chàirn or the col between Am Bodach and Sgùrr an
Iubhair. Both options leave you a long way from your
car, but there is a bus service between Fort William
and Kinlochleven. To extend the adventure, add on
Stob Bàn or try the full Tour of the Mamores route.

RACE The Salomon Ring of Steall Skyrace (29 kilometres
with 2,500 metres of ascent) takes an alternative and
longer route which starts and finishes in Kinlochleven.
Course records are held by (F) Judith Wyder with
3 hours and 36 minutes in 2019 and (M) Kilian Jornet
with 3 hours and 4 minutes in 2018. For more information or to enter, visit *www.skylinescotland.com*

WHAT NEXT? Alternative mountain rounds in Scotland
include the South Glen Shiel Ridge (see page 98)
or the Creag Meagaidh Traverse in Highland; the
Lawers Range in Perth and Kinross; or the wonderful
Fisherfield Munros. You can then build up to the
Fannaichs or the Mullardoch Round in Highland.
For a similar but longer route check out the Lochaber
Traverse (see page 104) or the harder Salomon Glen
Coe Skyline route.

Elsewhere in Great Britain, run the Snowdon
SkyRace route, any of the great Lakeland horseshoes,
the Langdale Skyline (see page 32) or the Brecon
Beacons Horseshoe.

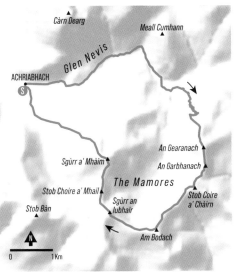

Càrn Dearg

Meall Cumhann

Glen Nevis

ACHRIABHACH

S

An Gearanach

Sgùrr a' Mhàim

An Garbhanach

The Mamores

Stob Choire a' Mhail

Stob Coire a' Chàirn

Stob Bàn

Sgùrr an Iubhair

Am Bodach

N

0   1 Km

ALL PHOTOS, INCLUDING OVERLEAF © KERI WALLACE

1099m

52m

0km   17km

54
LAIRIG GHRU

31km | **FELL** | **NAVIGATION** 2 partial waymarking
EASTERN SCOTLAND AND THE CAIRNGORMS

A traverse of Scotland's most famous
mountain pass, bisecting the Cairngorms
National Park.

DISTANCE **31km** ASCENT **660m** TIME **3:30–5:30 hours**
START **Coylumbridge, near Aviemore** FINISH **Linn of Dee, near Braemar**
GRID REF **NH 914 106/NO 063 898** GPS **57.1741, -3.7966/56.9898, -3.5436**
PUBLIC TRANSPORT **There is no bus link between Braemar and
Aviemore, so the easiest option is to arrange a collection or run as a
pair, dropping one vehicle at the end before starting. An alternative is
to stay locally overnight and return via a different route the next day
– this has all the hallmarks of an epic weekend!** PARKING **Lay-by
parking (free) in Coylumbridge; Linn of Dee National Trust for Scotland
car park at the finish (parking charges apply for non-members)**

The Lairig Ghru is a deep pass through the central
Cairngorms, which has been used by people to travel
between Strathspey and Deeside for centuries; it was
used as a drovers' road as late as the 1870s. To traverse
this great cleft is a classic Scottish journey and a
popular trail race too.

The Lairig Ghru can be completed in either direction
(described north to south here).

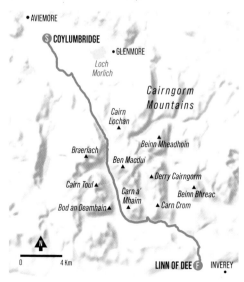

From Coylumbridge, immaculate trails lead through
ancient Caledonian pine forest, passing the Iron Bridge
(Cairngorm Club Footbridge) to the crossroads known
as Piccadilly. From here, a trail signposted to Lairig Ghru
climbs up until you are running inside the great pass,
with crags and cliffs on both sides. The trail is clearly
visible until you approach the high point of the route
which is characterised by stony moraines left behind by
a glacier. Here you will need to do some boulder-hopping
until you reach two small lochans known as the Pools
of Dee (the highest point of the pass is 835 metres).

Beyond this, the trail gradually reappears as the angle
eases and you can enjoy spectacular trail running and
scenery as you descend the lairig, passing Corrour bothy
and traversing east round the lower slopes of Carn a'
Mhaim. There is a ford (or a short detour to a footbridge)
at Glen Luibeg, then at the derelict Derry Lodge, a broad
vehicle track leads down Glen Lui to the Linn of Dee.

OTHER OPTIONS Once committed to the Lairig Ghru there
is no easy escape. The main bail-out option is to turn
around. It is possible however, to shorten the overall
challenge slightly by starting at the Sugar Bowl car
park and joining the lairig by way of a steep-sided and
rocky channel known as the Chalamain Gap.

To extend the challenge, run a return journey from
Derry Lodge via Glen Derry and Lairig an Laoigh,
finishing over the Ryvoan Pass. This is an awesome
long-distance circuit, doable over one or two days.

RACE The Lairig Ghru Race takes a longer, 43-kilometre,
south-to-north route, linking the police stations in
Braemar and Aviemore. Race records are (F) Lucy
Colquhoun with 3 hours and 32 minutes in 2006;
(M) Murray Strain with 2 hours and 58 minutes
in 2017. For more information or to enter, visit
www.deesiderunners.com/races/lairig-ghru-race

WHAT NEXT? For a similar challenge try the section of
the West Highland Way from Bridge of Orchy to Fort
William or parts of the Cape Wrath Trail (sections
through Torridon or the Fisherfields). You could also
try the Nine Edges route in the Peak District (see page
28) or rugged stretches of the Pennine Way (near
Malham Cove or High Cup Nick).

© KERI WALLACE

55

SUILVEN

20km | **MOUNTAIN** | **NAVIGATION** 4 difficult self-navigation or complex terrain
NORTH WEST HIGHLANDS

Stand on the summit of this remote peak –
a much-sought-after prize with one of the
most spectacular views in Scotland.

DISTANCE **20km** ASCENT **750m** TIME **3:30–5 hours**
START/FINISH **End of public road from Lochinver heading towards**
Glencanisp Lodge GRID REF **NC 107 219** GPS **58.1460, -5.2173**
PUBLIC TRANSPORT **No practical options** PARKING **Lay-by parking**
(donation box), or park in Lochinver (2km west of the start point)

Although Suilven is only 731 metres high, it is one
of Scotland's most desirable summits. Its shapely
bulk of Torridonian sandstone towers dramatically
above a bedrock of Lewisian gneiss – some of the
oldest rock in Western Europe. The mountain carves
a mesmerising outline in the vast, open landscape of
Sutherland.

Right from the start, you have your goal of Suilven
before your eyes. From the road end, the route passes
the Suileag bothy turn-off, following the river until a
less obvious but well-made path leads off right, heading
directly for Suilven. This wonderful path weaves
through lochans and rocky outcrops, heading up
between Loch na Barrack and Loch a' Choire Dubh.

Now the route begins to climb in earnest, ascending
steeply up a grassy gully to the cut-in col between
Caisteal Liath at the western end of the ridge and Meall
Meadhonach at the eastern end. As you arrive at the
col, a breathtaking view suddenly appears before you.
Once you recover, the trail leads through a gap in a
drystone wall and up towards the true summit via a
number of rocky steps (easy scrambling). The ridge
levels off briefly before the final climb to the rounded
summit of Suilven. At the top, turn around to take in
the fantastic view back along the ridge to the spire of
Meall Meadhonach. Return the same way.

OTHER OPTIONS To extend, add in an out-and-back to
Meall Meadhonach and the craggy east top of Meall
Beag by scrambling (grade 3) along the spine of the
mountain.

The central col can also be reached from
Inverkirkaig, by running past the Falls of Kirkaig and
along the northern side of Fionn Loch. This route is
arguably a more impressive approach, but the trail
is of a lower quality.

Combine Suilven with an ascent of Canisp for
a bigger version of this challenge.

WHAT NEXT? For something similar in Scotland, try Ben
Vrackie in Perth and Kinross; Arkle in Sutherland;
or Beinn Resipol in Sunart. To try something bigger,
consider the Munros Buachaille Etive Mòr in Glen
Coe; Beinn Eighe in Wester Ross; Ladhar Bheinn in
Knoydart; or Ben Alder in Highland. If it's the harder
scrambling you're into, then the fantastic Clach Glas
to Blà Bheinn traverse on Skye is a must-do. Elsewhere
in Great Britain, add Tryfan or Cadair Idris (see page
144) in Eryri and Helvellyn (see page 11) or Steeple in
the Lake District to your ticklist.

56
WHITE MOUNTH MUNROS

29km | FELL | NAVIGATION 3 no waymarking
EASTERN SCOTLAND AND THE CAIRNGORMS

A terrific high-level circuit, taking in five
Munros surrounding Loch Muick, including
Lochnagar with its spectacular northern coire.

DISTANCE **29km** ASCENT **1,060m** TIME **4–6 hours**
START/FINISH **Spittal of Glenmuick** GRID REF **NO 309 851**
GPS **56.9525, -3.1360** PUBLIC TRANSPORT **No practical options**
PARKING **Spittal of Glenmuick car park (parking charges apply)**

The impressive mountain of Lochnagar – also known
as Beinn Chiochan – stands guard over Balmoral
Castle and the towns of Royal Deeside. The circuit
over its summit and around beautiful Loch Muick
is popular with runners as it crosses an amenable,
flowing plateau with expansive views but also offers
proximity to several dramatic cliffs and coires.

There is a good track from the Spittal of Glenmuick
up through forestry to a cairn which marks the turning
point to Lochnagar. Pleasant running leads up on to
the plateau, with views of Lochnagar's spectacular
northern coire. From the cairn marking Cac Càrn Mòr
there's an out-and-back to Cac Carn Beag, Lochnagar's
highest point. If it is clear, you can see Deeside and the
Cairngorms massif from here (if not, you are in good
company with Queen Victoria). The route hugs the cliff
edge round to Carn a' Choire Bhoidheach and across
to two-cairned Càrn an t-Sagairt Mòr. Just to the north
is the scattered wreckage of a Canberra aircraft that

crashed here in 1956, including a large section of wing.

From here, the route heads south-east across a
runnable wide bealach and over Cairn Bannoch and
Broad Cairn, high above the dark waters of Dubh Loch.
It's then downhill over Little Craig to reach a col before
turning north-east and following the slopes above Loch
Muick. The trail weaves down to its southern shore
where a pleasant lochside trail leads back to the car park.

GOOD TO KNOW The challenge is described here in an anticlockwise direction, but should be reversed in north-
easterly winds due to the strong wind-funnelling effect
created by Loch Muick. Take extra care on the summit
plateau in poor visibility; there are few obvious
features and the cliffs are steep on the northern edge.

OTHER OPTIONS To bail out from Lochnagar, head south-
east off the summit and drop into the coire below to
follow the Glas Allt. The trail passes by Falls of the
Glasallt, then drops steeply down to the northern
shore of Loch Muick. Turn left and follow the shoreline
via the Boat House, back to the start.

Compared to the great cliffs of Lochnagar, the lesser-
known Creag an Dubh-loch is just as remarkable,
and well worth an out-and-back run from the Spittal
of Glenmuick, if seeking a lower-level outing.

WHAT NEXT? For other big Munro-bagging circuits check-
out the nearby Glen Clova Munros, the Glenshee 9
or the Cairngorm 4000s (see page 108). Further afield
try the Fannaichs, the South Glen Shiel Ridge (see
page 98) or the Fisherfield Munros.

57
RUM CUILLIN

22km | **MOUNTAIN** | **NAVIGATION** **4** difficult self-navigation or complex terrain
INNER HEBRIDES

A demanding circular mountain run which visits all five of the major peaks on Rum, with incredible views of the Hebrides.

DISTANCE **22km** ASCENT **1,430m** TIME **4–6 hours** START/FINISH
Kinloch Castle, Kinloch GRID REF **NM 401 995** GPS **57.0132, -6.2829**
PUBLIC TRANSPORT **Rum can be reached by a ferry from Mallaig on the mainland. The start of the route is a short walk from the ferry terminal**

Rum is the largest of the Small Isles of the Inner Hebrides. Its rugged peaks would surely be more popular if they weren't so close to the larger Skye Cuillin. By comparison, the Rum Cuillin offer a wilder, quieter and more esoteric adventure, with equally splendid scenery.

Once on the main ridge, easy scrambling leads to a 518-metre top, then up rocky ground beloved by snacking eagles to the main 722-metre summit of Hallival. You then follow the ridge down to a broad bealach before climbing a grassy ridgeline to meet the wall of Askival's Pinnacle. Most of the difficulties can be avoided to the left (east) – the trail is sometimes exposed but not difficult, though there is an 'interesting' move to reach the summit itself. The holes in the ground are the nesting burrows of Manx shearwater, and you may hear them shrieking underground. Norse settlers thought the noise was trolls, giving Trollabhal its name. Its rocky twin peaks give a fantastic easy scramble and the out-and-back detour to the west summit offers impressive views to Harris Bay.

There's a steep descent via a small gully and scree before you can weave up the ridge to summit Ainshval. Not far beyond, a grassy ridge leads to Sgùrr nan Gillean. Save some brainpower for the steep descent to Dibidil bothy, as care is needed to avoid the crags. It is then necessary to ford the Dibidil River, which is dangerous in spate. The damp path back to the village is compensated by exceptional views out to Eigg and Skye.

GOOD TO KNOW The route can be completed as a day trip but requires careful planning around the limited ferry timings – it is more relaxed to have an overnight stay on the island. The scrambling is mostly grade 1 or 2, but there is a section of moderate climbing if the Askival ridge is taken direct (it is mainly avoidable – see left).

OTHER OPTIONS This committing route has little water and limited escape routes after the dam in Coire Dubh. One possibility is to drop west from Bealach an Fhuarain towards Loch Fiachanais. From here you can reach Harris Bay and run via road back to the start.

Descend to Glen Dibidil from Bealach an Oir to refill on water or break the route into two shorter days, perhaps bivvying or descending to Dibidil bothy, a Mountain Bothies Association refuge, *www.mountainbothies.org.uk*

WHAT NEXT? If you enjoyed the Rum Cuillin then why not try the Paps of Jura (see page 78) or some of the mountains in the Skye Cuillin. Other great mountain running days out with grade-2 scrambling in Scotland include the Aonach Eagach traverse in Glen Coe and the Liathach traverse or the An Teallach ridge (grade 2 but 3 if taken directly) in Wester Ross. Elsewhere, try the Rab Pinnacle Ridge Extreme race route (Pinnacle Ridge is a grade-3 scramble) in the Lake District; and the Snowdon SkyRace route or the Bochlwyd Horseshoe (including Tryfan and Bristly Ridge) in Eryri.

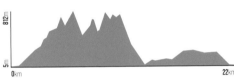

KINLOCH   Loch Scresort

Barkeval

Isle of
Rum

Hallival

Trollabhal

Askival

Clough's
Crag

Ainshval

Beinn nan Stac

Leac a' Chaisteil

Sgùrr nan
Gillean

N

0   2 Km

58
OCHIL 2000s

34km | **FELL** | **NAVIGATION** 2 partial waymarking
CENTRAL AND SOUTHERN SCOTLAND

An accessible and popular challenge linking the 2,000-foot Ochil summits, undulating from Glen Devon to the University of Stirling.

This challenge is a runnable peak-bagging challenge over rolling terrain, as well as a much-loved fell race that will test your navigation skills in the second half.

The route heads through the forest and then you can get started on the peak bagging, knocking off Innerdownie (the lowest of the 2000s), Bentie Knowe, Whitewisp Hill and Tarmangie Hill in turn. Hefty King's Seat Hill leads on to Andrew Gannel Hill, an out-and-back for The Law, then on to Ben Cleuch, the highest hill in the Ochil range.

In low visibility, navigation becomes more challenging from Ben Buck onwards, with fewer obvious features as a guide. Tick off Ben Ever, then strike out boldly through the peat hags to Blairdenon Hill. This is the last of the 2000s but you can swing by the bonus hill of Dumyat (a source of agates) with its characteristic shape and ruined hillfort, before following the tourist path to Yellowcraig Wood, and dashing towards the loch in the University of Stirling grounds.

OTHER OPTIONS For a short challenge, run up the popular peak of Dumyat from the university grounds (as per the popular Dumyat Hill Race). A circular route over the Ochil 2000s summits is also possible from Ochil Hills Woodland Park – it is slightly longer than the race route.

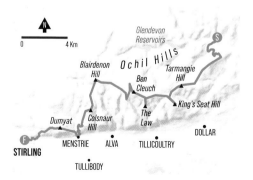

DISTANCE **34km** ASCENT **1,300m** TIME **4–6 hours** START **Glensherup Reservoir car park** FINISH **Loch Airthrey, University of Stirling** GRID REF **NN 971 051/NS 805 966** GPS **56.2277, -3.6598/56.1479, -3.9242** PUBLIC TRANSPORT **Stirling has good bus and rail connections; there is no public transport to the start point. On race day a bus takes competitors from the university to the start. On other days you'll have to arrange to get dropped off** PARKING **Glensherup Reservoir car park (free)**

ULTRA ROUTE For a longer challenge, Wee Run Events organises three events through the Ochil Hills – the Ochil Ultra short (30 miles), the Ochil Ultra (50 miles) and the Ochil 100, *www.ochilultra.run*

RACE The Ochil 2000s race is organised by Ochil Hill Runners, *www.ochilhillrunners.org.uk* Course records belong to (F) Catriona Buchanan at 3:20.55 in 2018 and (M) Kris Jones at 02:47.44 in 2023.

WHAT NEXT? Other similar Scottish hill races include the Glenshee 9 and the Two Breweries Hill Race. For comparable Category A long fell races consider the Llangollen Fell Race (see page 146), Helvellyn and the Dodds Race, Don Morrison Memorial Edale Skyline fell race, Duddon Valley Fell Race or the Sheeptracks (part of the Clwydian Fell Race).

59

PENTLAND SKYLINE

28km | **TRAIL** | **NAVIGATION 3** no waymarking
CENTRAL AND SOUTHERN SCOTLAND

Follow the route of the Pentland Skyline Race, ticking all the main summits in the Pentland Hills.

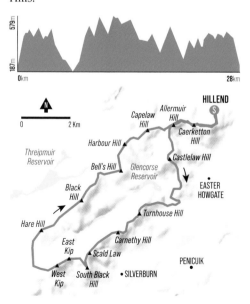

DISTANCE **28km** ASCENT **1,400m** TIME **4:00–5:45 hours** RECORDS **(F) A. Mudge 2:42.29 in 2002; (M) Kris Jones 2:15.52 in 2016** START/FINISH **Midlothian Snowsports Centre, Hillend** GRID REF **NT 243 667** GPS **55.8875, -3.2105** PUBLIC TRANSPORT **Regular buses run between Edinburgh and Hillend** PARKING **Hillend Upper car park (free)**

The Pentland Skyline Race was first run in 1986 and is now a popular and fast trail race over rolling hills which can be seen from the city of Edinburgh. Often billed as a race of two halves, the first section of this challenge covers runnable grassy terrain with good trails. The return leg from the Drove Road is over rougher ground and is much tougher.

After a steep initial climb up a grassy trod directly to the summit of Caerketton Hill, a runnable rollercoaster follows, as you head over Castlelaw Hill, accompanied by the sound of the military rifle ranges, then Turnhouse Hill and Carnethy Hill. There is a slight diversion from the main ridge, running over grass and peat to tick off South Black Hill. After taking the main path over the Kips, you leave the trail again to reach the summit of Hare Hill. Rough, boggy and vegetated terrain along the ridge is eventually alleviated by a pleasant grassy climb up to the summit of Bell's Hill. The trail becomes more obvious here and can be followed easily over the final summits and back to the start.

Though less grand than some of the rounds of the high mountains, this one has a charm all of its own. The hills are just the right size, perfectly graded for enjoyable running.

OTHER OPTIONS This route can be shortened either by taking the trail north-west from between Carnethy Hill and Scald Law, or south-east from between Hare Hill and Black Hill, towards The Howe, and then along the track linking Loganlee and Glencorse reservoirs. There are a great many options for linking hills in the Pentlands and a good map of all these is available through the Pentland Hills Regional Park website: *www.pentlandhills.org*

RACE The Pentland Skyline Race and shorter races such as the Carnethy 5 are organised by the Carnethy Hill Running Club. There have recently been some access issues for the race, but individual runners can access the area without issues.

WHAT NEXT? For a similar challenge you could try the Sedbergh Hills Fell Race route, the Ochil 2000s (see page 92), the Glenshee 9 or the Edale Skyline (see page 24). For bigger hills try a traverse of the higher Lawers Range in Perth and Kinross; the Fairfield Horseshoe Fell Race route in the Lake District; or the Carneddau ridge from the Ogwen Valley in Eryri.

60
THE ARRAN CORBETTS

25km | MOUNTAIN | NAVIGATION 4 difficult self-navigation or complex terrain
CENTRAL AND SOUTHERN SCOTLAND

Combining the well-known Goatfell with its three neighbouring Corbetts creates a circuit of technical peaks with outstanding views across the Isle of Arran.

> DISTANCE **25km** ASCENT **1,640m** TIME **4:30–6:30 hours** START/FINISH **Cladach, near Brodick** GRID REF **NS 012 375** GPS **55.5912, -5.1555** PUBLIC TRANSPORT **There are two ferries to Arran: Ardrossan to Brodick or Claonaig in Kintyre to Lochranza, www.calmac.co.uk** PARKING **Various options available in Cladach and Brodick**

Discover Scotland in miniature and explore majestic granite peaks in the National Scenic Area of North Arran – an unforgettable island experience, just a stone's throw from Glasgow.

The route starts with a bit of road running from Cladach, then up the minor road to Glen Rosa. The first climb is up Beinn Nuis via its south-east ridge before heading north to Beinn Tarsuinn. Just before the final ascent to the summit of Beinn Tarsuinn, look out on your right for the Old Man of Tarsuinn – a rocky outcrop resembling a human profile looking out to sea. The route now drops down to avoid graded rock climbing along the ridge crest, missing out the summit of A' Chir altogether (it's not a Corbett after all). After an easy out-and-back on grass to the summit of Caisteal Abhail, carry on to enjoy Cir Mhòr's summit with its striking pinnacle and remarkable, airy views.

The scramble down the east ridge to The Saddle is exposed. (For an easier option, return to the col between Cir Mhòr and A' Chir before dropping into the coire to skirt east (faint path) traversing around under Cir Mhòr to The Saddle.) The ridge continues round to North Goatfell and then Goatfell, a popular Corbett with panoramic views. The return route is via a well-defined tourist path back to Cladach.

OTHER OPTIONS A slightly shorter but equally challenging route with a more demanding scrambling is the Sannox Horseshoe on Arran; it links Cioch na h-Oighe, The Saddle, Cir Mhòr and Caisteal Abhail around Glen Sannox (15 kilometres with 1,700 metres of ascent).

The simplest summit objective is a straight out-and-back ascent of Goatfell via the tourist trail from Cladach.

ULTRA ROUTE Arran is home to the two-day Ultra Tour of Arran from Rat Race events, *www.ultratourofarran.co.uk*

RACE The Goatfell Hill Race, organised by Shettleston Harriers, is a classic. Sadly, the excellent Glen Rosa Horseshoe race has now been discontinued.

WHAT NEXT? To explore the island further, try a round of the far quieter Pirnmill Hills or the Arran Coastal Way, which takes in highlights such as Goatfell's summit, the remote Cock of Arran, King's Cave and picturesque Lamlash Bay.

For similar technical mountain rounds elsewhere, try the Ring of Steall (see page 82); the Ben Cruachan Horseshoe in the Southern Highlands; Beinn Alligin or the Liathach Traverse in Wester Ross; the Three Sisters of Glencoe (Bidean Circuit) or the Fisherfield Munros; the Tarmachan Ridge in Perth and Kinross; the Helvellyn Edges in the Lake District (see page 11); the Yr Wyddfa/Snowdon Horseshoe in Eryri (see page 136); or the Glyderau in Eryri.

61

SOUTH GLEN SHIEL RIDGE

27km | FELL | NAVIGATION 4 difficult self-navigation
or complex terrain
WESTERN HIGHLANDS

Traverse a chain of seven runnable Munros
with views to Knoydart, Skye and Torridon.

DISTANCE **27km** ASCENT **1,610m** TIME **4:30–6:30 hours**
START **Malagan Bridge lay-by, A87** FINISH **Cluanie Inn, A87**
GRID REF **NG 973 137/NH 077 117** GPS **57.1700, -5.3540/57.1564, -5.1808**
PUBLIC TRANSPORT **Bus services from both Edinburgh and Glasgow
to Portree pass through Glen Shiel. You will need to ask the driver for
an unscheduled stop at Malagan Bridge, www.citylink.co.uk**
PARKING **Lay-by parking on the A87 (free)**

For Munro baggers, this ridge can be very efficient,
as little height is lost between the summits. A steep
climb alongside the Allt Mhàlagain takes you up on
to the ridge; once on the ridge, fenceposts and walls
aid navigation as you summit each Munro in turn.
The true summit of Sgùrr an Doire Leathain requires
a slight detour north-east, but gives an excellent view
back to Creag nan Damh – the first Munro on the
ridge – all the way to Sgùrr Coire na Feinne (a lesser
summit which is actually bypassed by this route).

There is a bigger climb to the top of Aonach air Chrith,
the highest peak on this challenge, then the ridge
undulates with steep cliffs on its northern side until it
funnels you up on to the shoulder of Druim Shionnach.
Further east the ridge becomes very rocky and narrow,
but this tricky section can be bypassed by a trail on the
right. The final Munro of the day is Creag a' Mhàim.

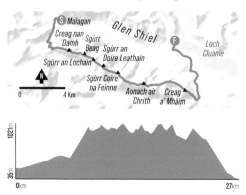

A trail to the south-east loses height quickly,
depositing you at the foot of the ridge, where the
stalkers' path brings you on to a large access track and
easy downhill trail running skirting the foothills above
the shore of Loch Cluanie. From there it is not far
before you arrive at the inn for a celebratory pint.

GOOD TO KNOW The start and finish are 12 kilometres
apart along the A87. An easy option is to leave a bike
at the Cluanie Inn. Running west to east allows for a
pub finish and a downhill 'roll' by bike back to your car.

OTHER OPTIONS To bail from the ridge there are several
(all steep) descents along its length. The safest option
is down Druim Coire nan Eirecheanach, heading north
from the subsidiary summit (981 metres) between
Sgùrr Coire na Feinne and Maol Chinn-dearg. It is also
possible to descend the north ridge of Sgùrr Coire na
Feinne (down Druim Thollaidh), where there are some
short easy scrambles.

The overall challenge can be extended by ascending
the Forcan Ridge (grade-2 scramble) and adding The
Saddle and Sgùrr na Sgine at the start of the described
route.

ULTRA ROUTE The hills of the South Glen Shiel Ridge are
the first part of the Broxap Round, a 126-kilometre
round (with over 10,000 metres of ascent) created by
Jon Broxap in 1988 during which he broke the 24-hour
Munro record of the time. The record now stands at 33
Munros (Kim Collinson, 2021) but the Broxap Round

remains an epic challenge in its own right. The Broxap Round starts and finishes at the Cluanie Inn.

In 2021, Finlay Wild completed a Glen Shiel Round in 8 hours and 47 minutes. His route covered 56 kilometres with 5,500 metres of ascent – it makes for an attractive and logical round of the Munro summits on both sides of the glen, *www.gomountaingoats.com/ words/glen-shiel-round*

WHAT NEXT? If you like this kind of gradually undulating fell running then you should try a traverse of Creag Meagaidh in Highland; the White Mounth Munros in the Cairngorms (see page 89); Glenshee 9 hill race; or the Lawers Range in Perth and Kinross. Outside of Scotland take a look at the Helvellyn and the Dodds Race in the Lake District; the Edale Skyline (see page 24) or the Kinder Plateau perimeter in the Peak District; or a Carneddau circuit in Eryri.

62
TROTTERNISH RIDGE

30km | **FELL** | **NAVIGATION** 4 difficult self-navigation
or complex terrain
SKYE

A runnable high-level traverse linking weird
and wonderful rock formations from the
Quiraing to The Storr on this unique section
of the Skye Trail.

DISTANCE **30km**   ASCENT **1,420m**   TIME **4:30–6:30 hours**
START **Flodigarry**   FINISH **Old Man of Storr car park**   GRID REF **NG 462 718/
NG 509 529**   GPS **57.6644, -6.2566/57.4977, -6.1590**   PUBLIC TRANSPORT
The start and finish are 23 kilometres apart on the A855. Stagecoach
57A runs between the Old Man of Storr car park and Flodigarry – catch
a bus to the start and run back to your car   PARKING **Lay-by parking at
the start (free; please park considerately); Old Man of Storr car park
at the finish (parking charges apply)**

The Trotternish Ridge is one of the finest traverses
in Britain and is simply unique in every respect – a
justifiably popular section of the Skye Trail. Highlights
includes the quirky Quiraing and striking Old Man of
Storr, both of which are shrouded in legend and attract
many tourists to Skye each year.

   The route starts from Flodigarry and heads south,
up below the dramatic cliffs of the Quiraing and
passing the triple summit of The Prison on the
left and the obvious detached Needle on the right.

   Once across the road, the trail takes to the cliffs
above the escarpment, climbing Bioda Buidhe and
continuing south with a long steady climb up the flank
of Beinn Edra, whose summit keeps its charms hidden
until the very last minute, then continuing gently over
Beinn Mheadhonach, Groba nan Each, Flasvein and

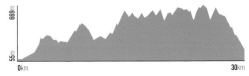

Creag a' Lain before climbing Sgùrr a' Mhadaidh Ruaidh (the Peak of the Red Fox) via a narrow grassy neck. The route then follows the edge of the escarpment to ascend the higher peak of Baca Ruadh and the summit of Hartaval. Beware high winds at the cliff edges.

Climbing The Storr is an optional extra out-and-back, as the route begins to descend from the ridge just before it, cutting down to traverse the north-east-facing coire below the summit. There is a brief rocky scramble, after which the trail becomes clearer, and you can enjoy the sight of the iconic Old Man of Storr (a prominent pinnacle of rock) on your way to the finish.

OTHER OPTIONS The Skye Trail breaks into seven recognised stages, each of which makes for an interesting run in its own right. The section from Sligachan to Elgol is of particular note, with its rugged feel and fantastic views of the Skye Cuillin.

ULTRA ROUTE The Skye Trail is an unofficial long-distance trail showcasing 128 kilometres of spectacular but tough terrain across Skye, from Broadford to Rubha

Hunish. Much of the route is challenging and pathless (not waymarked).

RACE The Trotternish Ridge Race is a traditional category A long fell race along this section of the Skye Trail. There is also the Skye Trail Ultra, an event running the full length of the trail, excluding the Rubha Hunish headland, *www.skyetrailultra.uk* Course records belong to (F) Caroline MacKay at 17:00.00 in 2015 and (M) Jeremy Cottingham at 13:50.00 in 2022.

WHAT NEXT? For similar fascinating terrain visit Suilven (see page 88), Stac Pollaidh or do the Foinaven Circuit (see page 74) in the North West Highlands; Duncansby Head on the north-east tip of the mainland; The Cobbler in Loch Lomond and the Trossachs; the Whangie in Stirling; or the Inverailort or Applecross Corbetts in the Western Highlands. A similar scale of wonder can be found along the Cape Wrath Trail. Challenges elsewhere in Great Britain that might be of interest include dramatic sections of the Pennine Way and the South West Coast Path.

63

ST JOHN'S TOWN OF DALRY TO SANQUHAR

42km | TRAIL | NAVIGATION 1 fully waymarked
CENTRAL AND SOUTHERN SCOTLAND

DISTANCE **42km** ASCENT **960m** TIME **5–7 hours** START St John's Town of Dalry FINISH Sanquhar GRID REF **NX 619 811/NS 781 099** GPS **55.1058, -4.1651/55.3679, -3.9247** PUBLIC TRANSPORT **Frequent buses and trains between Sanquhar and Dumfries, then infrequent buses on to St John's Town of Dalry** PARKING **On-street parking in St John's Town of Dalry and Sanquhar**

A long and remote section of Scotland's official coast-to-coast route, the Southern Upland Way, traversing exposed moorland and quiet hills of The Glenkens.

From St John's Town of Dalry, start by passing through farmland and forestry, before climbing the heathery slopes of Benbrack. On the summit is a huge red sandstone arch, one of Andy Goldsworth's Striding Arches. From here the route follows a moorland ridge above the trees to Cairn Hill and Black Hill, then heads along the forest edge to High Countam. The trail then dives into the forest (this section can be boggy), passing Allan's Cairn, a memorial to Covenanters killed during the 1680s, before emerging near Polskeoch bothy.

From the bothy, a short road section leads you to Polgown, where you leave the road for a climb up Cloud Hill, which has fine views of the rest of the way to Sanquhar. There's a Southern Upland Way information shelter beside the Blackaddie Bridge and the town has plenty of cosy cafes where you can warm up if necessary!

OTHER OPTIONS End your challenge early at any of the road crossings.

Each section of the Southern Upland Way makes for an enjoyable linear run in its own right. Check out the coastal path section at Portpatrick; the Lowther Hills section just north of Sanquhar; the high-level section through the Ettrick Hills near Peebles; or the Lammermuir Hills section south of Edinburgh.

ULTRA ROUTE The Southern Upland Way is Scotland's official coast-to-coast route; it is 344 kilometres long with around 8,000 metres of ascent. Linking Portpatrick on the west coast to Cockburnspath on the east, it is waymarked throughout. Opened in 1984, the exact route of the Way has evolved over the years to reflect changes in the landscape and local communities. The FKTs belong to (F) Joasia Zakrzewski with 2:14:20.45 in 2021 and (M) Jack Scott with 2:07:42.42 in 2020.

RACE The Race Across Scotland is a supported ultra-trail race along the full length of the Southern Upland Way, organised by GB Ultras. *www.gbultras.com*

WHAT NEXT? For a more accessible or shorter long-distance coast-to-coast challenge in Scotland, try the John Muir Way or the Great Glen Way. For something more demanding, you might consider the Wainwright's Coast to Coast trail in Northern England. For a similar scale and more famous challenge, try the Pennine Way.

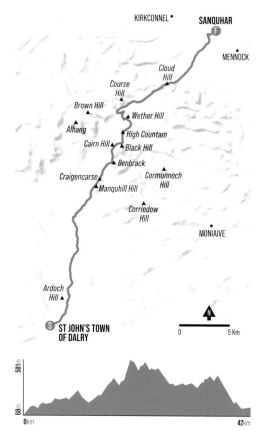

64

LOCHABER TRAVERSE

30km | MOUNTAIN | NAVIGATION 4 difficult self-navigation or complex terrain
WESTERN HIGHLANDS

The ultimate high-level traverse in the Western Highlands crossing six Munros before a spectacular finale on the seventh – Ben Nevis.

DISTANCE **30km** ASCENT **2,370m** TIME **5-7 hours** RECORDS **(F) Georgia Tindley 5:33.29 in 2020; (M) Finlay Wild 3:23.53 in 2023** START **Wee Minister sculpture near Corriechoille** FINISH **Glen Nevis** GRID REF **NN 257 787/NN 125 729** GPS **56.8668, -4.8610/56.8104, -5.0717** PUBLIC TRANSPORT **No practical options** PARKING **Limited lay-by parking near Corriechoille and some lay-by parking in Glen Nevis; park considerately - do not block any gates or farm tracks**

The Lochaber Traverse offers fantastic technical running and scrambling, culminating with the UK's highest peak. Although this challenge can be completed in either direction, the east–west traverse is most popular due to the aesthetic appeal of finishing with Ben Nevis.

The route crosses the rooftop of the West Highlands, traversing the Grey Corries, the two Aonachs and Ben Nevis, which is reached via the popular grade 1 scramble up the Carn Mòr Dearg Arête, which gives stunning views of the mountain's corrugated north face, a climbers' paradise.

Clock-chasers can stop their watches on the bridge over the River Nevis in order to avoid sprinting across the busy road.

ALL PHOTOS © KERI WALLACE

This route was done as a 'rest day' by the famous Scottish climbing partnership of Robin Smith and Jimmy Marshall, in the week that they transformed Scottish winter mountaineering by climbing several new cutting-edge routes on Ben Nevis's north face.

OTHER OPTIONS The Grey Corries Traverse makes for a great horseshoe in its own right. Ben Nevis and Càrn Mòr Dearg also form a popular horseshoe route (descend over Càrn Dearg Meadhonach and then down to the CIC Hut track).

The two low-level bealachs separating Ben Nevis from the Aonachs, and the Aonachs from the Grey Corries, provide the most obvious bail-out options.

RACE Ben Nevis is home to the historic Ben Nevis Race, first held in 1951. Race records belong to (F) Victoria Wilkinson with 1:43.01 in 2018 and (M) Kenny Stuart with 1:25.34 in 1984.

WHAT NEXT? For a similar challenge in the same area try the Mamores Round or combine the two to make a full Tranter's Round. For a more technical challenge, consider the Glen Coe Skyline race route or the traditional Glen Coe Round. Another great option is the Martin Moran Round. Elsewhere, the Welsh 3000s (see page 156), the Lake District 3000s and Cumbrian Traverse (see page 42) are comparable great challenges.

65
KNOYDART TRAVERSE

46km | **FELL** | **NAVIGATION** 3 no waymarking
WESTERN HIGHLANDS

A spectacular traverse of Scotland's 'Last
Wilderness', the Rough Bounds of Knoydart.

DISTANCE **46km** ASCENT **1,450m** TIME **6-8 hours** START **Inverie**
FINISH **Glenfinnan** GRID REF **NG 764 002/NM 905 808**
GPS **57.0385, -5.6858/56.8714, -5.4381** PUBLIC TRANSPORT **Knoydart
is cut off from the UK mainland road network. Inverie can be reached
by train and ferry (via Mallaig); get the train home from Glenfinnan at
the end of your run** PARKING **Various options in Glenfinnan**

Knoydart is a community-owned, rugged landscape
of lochs and mountains, sandwiched between Loch
Nevis and Loch Hourn. To say these trails are remote is
an understatement and the linear challenge spanning
the peninsula requires self-reliance and a penchant
for solitude. Knoydart has a wild beauty, unparalleled
elsewhere in Great Britain. This challenge gives the
most accessible traverse of the peninsula, finishing
at Glenfinnan.

The start point at Inverie is the peninsula's only

© SHUTTERSTOCK/PETER SKELTON

village (home to what is said to be the most remote pub
in mainland Britain) and it just gets more remote from
there. However, the wilderness is alleviated by several
charming bothies – Sourlies, A'Chuil, and Corryhully –
before you pass beneath the iconic Glenfinnan Viaduct
to finish.

OTHER OPTIONS You can bail out early via Glen Dessarry to
the western end of the minor road along the northern
shore of Loch Arkaig (this is also a very remote location).
A branch of the Cape Wrath Trail offers an alter-

native route through Knoydart (Glenfinnan to Kinloch Hourn), and is taken on day two of the Cape Wrath Ultra (54 kilometres with 1,600 metres of ascent).

Trail running in Knoydart means considerable logistics, but any adventure in this wild and stunning landscape is worth the investment.

RACE The 125-kilometre Highland Ultra stage race take place around the Knoydart Peninsula over three days. For more information or to enter, visit *www.beyondtheultimate.co.uk*

WHAT NEXT? For other linear routes through remote landscapes in Scotland, take a look at sections of the Cape Wrath or Skye trails (see pages 76 and 100). For a day route, the Lairig Ghru (see page 86) is a similar but shorter experience. Many of Great Britain's long-distance trails have sections with remote terrain – try the Pennine Way or Wainwright's Coast to Coast in Northern England; or the Cambrian Way (see page 166).

66
CAIRNGORM 4000s

40km | **MOUNTAIN** | **NAVIGATION 4** difficult self-navigation or complex terrain
EASTERN SCOTLAND AND THE CAIRNGORMS

A stunning round of the 4,000-feet Munros in the Cairngorms National Park, crossing the vast Cairngorm plateau and striking Lairig Ghru pass.

DISTANCE **40km**   ASCENT **2,400m**   TIME **6:00–7:30 hours**
START/FINISH **Cairngorm Mountain Base Station**   GRID REF **NH 989 061**
GPS **57.1348, -3.6713**   PUBLIC TRANSPORT **Regular buses run between Aviemore and Cairngorm Mountain**   PARKING **Cairngorm Mountain Coire Cas car park (parking charges apply)**   MORE INFO **At the time of writing, the trail alongside the Allt a' Choire Chais between the Coire Cas car park and Utsi Bridge is closed due to subsidence and is unsafe**

This challenge was first conceived as a traverse of all Cairngorm Munros over 4,000 feet, which at the time were Cairn Gorm, Ben Macdui, Cairn Toul and Braeriach. Eric Beard recorded the first round of the four in 1963, but since Sgòr an Lochain Uaine (also known as The Angel's Peak) was promoted to Munro status in 1997, most runners now include all five summits. These five are the highest mountains in the British Isles after Ben Nevis, and the Cairngorm Plateau includes some of Britain's highest and most remote terrain, so this is a hefty challenge. It can be completed in either direction – either way, the big climb of the day is up Cairn Toul.

If going clockwise, there is a choice of line into the Lairig Ghru – either take the direct route, descending steeply on the left-hand side of the south-west ridge, through bouldery, heathery ground or opt for the easier but longer route that heads more south-east to the top of the Allt Clach nan Taillear, then follows it down.

It is a good idea to recce the section along weaving trails that cut off the switchbacks along the road between the Sugar Bowl car park and the Cairngorm Mountain Upper Cas car park. Care is also needed when navigating the section between Stob Coire an t-Sneachda and Ben Macdui in poor visibility, as well as on the descent from Ben Macdui (if going clockwise) and the summit of Braeriach where the spectacular cliffs gouge out the edge of the plateau. If tackling this route in winter, bear in mind that the Chalamain Gap is a terrain trap in times of high avalanche risk.

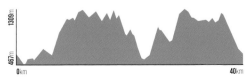

FKTs are recorded for the Cairngorm 4000s starting and finishing at Glenmore Lodge – (F) Caroline Marwick at 5:30.30 in 2020 and (M) Finlay Wild at 3:52.59 in 2018.

OTHER OPTIONS A loop around the Northern Corries (over Stob Coire an t-Sneachda and Cairn Lochan from the Cairngorm Mountain Base Station) is a great morning out. Another shorter alternative is to ascend only Cairn Gorm and Ben Macdui, then follow the Lairig Ghru south to the Chalamain Gap, considerably reducing the overall ascent of the day.

RACE There are several trail races and even a new ultra in the Cairngorms National Park but only the Lairig Ghru Race (see page 86) crosses the route of the 4000s, albeit briefly.

WHAT NEXT? For something similar in Scotland, you could try the Tour of the Mamores or a round of the White Mounth Munros or Glen Shiel (see pages 89 and 98) – or you could extend yourself with something more technical like the Tranter's Round. Elsewhere in Great Britain try George Fisher's Tea Round (see page 38) or the Cumbrian Traverse (see page 42) in the Lake District; the Yorkshire Three Peaks (see page 35); or the Welsh 3000s (see page 156).

BOTH PHOTOS © KERI WALLACE

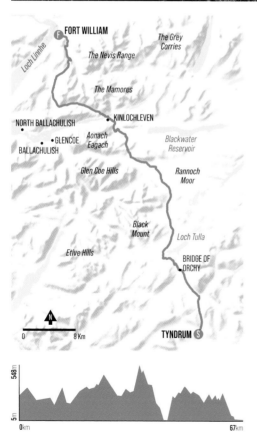

67
TYNDRUM TO FORT WILLIAM

67km | **TRAIL** | **NAVIGATION 1** *fully waymarked*
WESTERN HIGHLANDS

The northern half of the West Highland Way
from Tyndrum to Fort William is the most
challenging but also the most scenic stretch
of Scotland's oldest long-distance trail.

DISTANCE **67km** ASCENT **1,440m** TIME **8:30–10:30 hours**
START **Tyndrum** FINISH **Fort William** GRID REF **NN 328 306/NN 100 737**
GPS **56.4381, -4.7132/56.8162, -5.1140** PUBLIC TRANSPORT **Direct rail
and bus connections between Tyndrum and Fort William** PARKING
Various options available in Tyndrum and Fort William

The West Highland Way was first conceived by
a Glaswegian, Tom Hunter, and opened in 1980.
The national trail is now Scotland's oldest and
most popular long-distance journey. As such,
it's well waymarked throughout its length.

The route starts in Tyndrum, the smallest settlement
in Great Britain that has more than one railway station.
In the 19th century, the railway terminated here,

so visitors to Glen Coe had to finish their journey by cart. As you cross the wilderness of Rannoch Moor and approach the Kingshouse Hotel, you are taking the same route. At Altnafeadh, the trail veers away from the A82 and climbs the Devil's Staircase, the highest point on the West Highland Way at 548 metres. From here, there is a descent to Kinlochleven before a climb over Lairigmor then down in to Glen Nevis and on to the finish at Fort William.

OTHER OPTIONS This challenge can be split into four shorter sections – breaking at Inveroran, Kingshouse and Kinlochleven. Naturally, it is also possible to extend this route to include the southern sections from Milgnavie.

ULTRA ROUTE The full West Highland Way stretches 154 kilometres from Milngavie to Fort William, taking in a wide variety of scenery and terrain along the way – the annual West Highland Way Race follows this route.

RACE The Devil o' the Highlands Footrace covers the route described here. Course records belong to (F) Lucy Colquhoun at 5:47.28 in 2011 and (M) Rob Sinclair at 5:12.21 in 2017. For more information or to enter, see *www.devilothehighlandsfootrace.co.uk*

WHAT NEXT? You've tried south to north, so why not try coast to coast with the Southern Upland Way, or the wilds of the far north with the Cape Wrath Trail? Similar challenges elsewhere in Great Britain include the Pennine Way, the South Downs Way, the South West Coast Path or Offa's Dyke Path.

68
LOCH MULLARDOCH ROUND

57km | FELL | NAVIGATION 4 difficult self-navigation
or complex terrain
NORTH WEST HIGHLANDS

One of the biggest Munro-bagging challenges
in Scotland – this route links 12 Munros to
form a truly epic fell running circuit.

DISTANCE **57km** ASCENT **3,960m** TIME **12–16 hours** RECORDS **(F)**
Helen Bonsor 10:07 in 2018; (M) Finlay Wild 7:40 in 2020 START/FINISH
Mullardoch Dam GRID REF **NH 223 309** GPS **57.3346, -4.9537**
PUBLIC TRANSPORT **No practical options** PARKING **Mullardoch Dam
car park (free)**

A long-distance mountain round linking 12 runnable
Munros in the heart of the magnificent North West
Highlands. Some will wish to tackle this route over two
days while others should be prepared to run by headtorch!

The mountains around lonely Loch Mullardoch are
some of the wildest in Scotland and the ridges linking
them are unparalleled north of the Great Glen. The
route is long and committing and the only practical
escape is the purgatorial path along the northern bank
of Loch Mullardoch.

The views on the route, however, are stunning. From
the summit of An Riabhachan, steep slopes drop down
to the left, allowing you to glimpse Loch Mullardoch
and the Càrn Eighe range beyond it, but to the north
you can see most of Loch Monar, and a seemingly
endless array of peaks taking your gaze ever onward
into Torridon. Another highlight is An Socach, one of
the most remote Munros in Scotland, and a fabulous
vantage point at the heart of the North West Highlands,
from which you can enjoy views of Skye and the coast
as well as across its dramatic eastern corrie.

Finding water is a challenge on this route, but there
is a useful spring beside the path at around 950 metres
on the western flank of Sgùrr na Lapaich.

OTHER OPTIONS The round can be completed in a single
push or broken into smaller sections by bivvying along
the way.

Glen Affric Youth Hostel at Alltbeithe in nearby
Glen Affric can be used to extend this to a three-day
round (book in advance). Once committed to the
route there are limited easy escape options, however
it is possible to complete the northern Munros before
running back along the northern shore of Loch
Mullardoch. Alternatively, you can charter a boat
(google Loch Mullardoch Ferry Service) up the loch to
the foot of An Socach and run east along the northern
ridge for a shorter day.

Note that if retreating along the northern shore
of Loch Mullardoch, crossing the Allt Taige can be
difficult when in spate.

WHAT NEXT? Other large groups of Munros in Scotland
include Glen Shiel (both sides of the A87), the Cuillin
Ridge, the Fannaichs, Glenshee 9 and the Mamores 10.
Even bigger peak-bagging days in Great Britain include
the Lakes 24-hour round, 24-hour Munro round and
the UK Big Three.

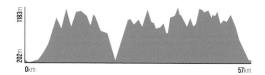

69
CHARLIE RAMSAY ROUND

94km | **MOUNTAIN** | **NAVIGATION** 4 difficult self-navigation or complex terrain
WESTERN HIGHLANDS

The definitive big mountain round of the Highlands – Scotland's answer to the Bob Graham Round – takes in 23 Munros including Ben Nevis.

DISTANCE **94km** ASCENT **6,950m** TIME **22–26 hours**
RECORDS **(F) Jasmin Paris 16:13.00 in 2016; (M) Finlay Wild 14:42.40 in 2020** START/FINISH **Glen Nevis Youth Hostel** GRID REF **NN 127 717**
GPS **56.7997, -5.0673** PUBLIC TRANSPORT **Buses run between Fort William and Glen Nevis. Fort William has both bus and rail links with the rest of Scotland** PARKING **Roadside parking and car parks in Glen Nevis (free/parking charge)**

The Charlie Ramsay Round was created and completed by its namesake in 1978. It was conceived by adding an extra leg to the existing Tranter's Round (created by Philip Tranter and Blyth Wright in 1964). The additional section added a further five Munros to the existing round, bringing it in line with the stats of its better-known Lake District equivalent, the Bob Graham Round.

Although usually regarded as a 24-hour fell running challenge, Charlie Ramsay is clear that any complete round should be hailed as a success, irrespective of time!

The round can be run in a clockwise or anticlockwise direction and takes in the Lochaber 4000s, the Grey Corries, the Fersit Hills and the Mamores. It is widely regarded as the most technical of the big three UK classic mountain rounds as there is sustained grade-1 scrambling on the Carn Mòr Dearg Arête and the Ring of Steall sections.

Unlike the Bob Graham Round, the Charlie Ramsay Round is only easily accessible (i.e. close to a road) at two points, making support more difficult. If one round isn't enough for you, follow Nicky Spinks's example – in 2018, she became the first ever person to run a double Ramsay Round in 55 hours and 56 minutes.

GOOD TO KNOW The Abhainn Rath can be difficult and dangerous to cross following heavy rain or a thaw.

OTHER OPTIONS The most obvious way to shorten the Charlie Ramsay Round is to run the Tranter's Round instead – this misses out the eastern section around Loch Treig. Tranter's Round covers 18 Munros over 59 kilometres with around 5,400 metres of ascent.

Leg 1 of the Charlie Ramsay Round from Glen Nevis to Fersit (or vice versa) is a good through route in its own right. It gives a good flavour of the whole round and includes the technical Carn Mòr Dearg Arête.

RACE Major events that take place along part of this route include the historic Ben Nevis Race, the Salomon Ben Nevis Ultra and the Salomon Ring of Steall Skyrace (the latter two are both part of the Skyline Scotland event series, *www.skylinescotland.com*).

WHAT NEXT? The Charlie Ramsay Round is one of the three big mountain rounds in Great Britain – the other two being the Bob Graham Round in England (see page 48) and the Paddy Buckley Round in Wales (see page 164). Alternative big mountain rounds in Scotland include the Broxap Round and the Martin Moran Round in the Western Highlands or the Rigby Round in the Cairngorms.

70
MUNRO ROUND

approximately 1,400km | FELL | NAVIGATION 4
difficult self-navigation or complex terrain
SCOTLAND

The ultimate Scottish peak-bagging challenge
– to complete all 282 of the country's Munros
(peaks over 3,000 feet) in a continuous push.

| DISTANCE **approximately 1,400km running (plus 1,400km cycling)**
| ASCENT **approximately 126,000m running (plus 14,250m cycling)**
| TIME **variable**   START/FINISH **anywhere**

The Munros were first listed by Sir Hugh Munro in his
Munro's Tables in 1891, which presented 283 'Munro
summits' (3,000 feet or higher), and another 255
additional summits greater than 3,000 feet considered
to be subsidiary 'Munro tops'. There are currently
282 Munro summits and 226 Munro Tops. The first
person to climb all these Munros was Reverend A.E.
Robertson in 1901 and by the late 1980s there had
been a considerable surge in the popularity of 'Munro-
bagging'. Those who climb all of the summits are
known as 'Compleators' or 'Munroists'.

   The original challenge was to bag all the peaks
within your lifetime, not in one continuous push.
The first recorded continuous round was completed
by mountaineer and author Hamish Brown over 112
days in 1974. More recently, the self-propelled record

was smashed by Donnie Campbell, who completed the round in 31 days, 23 hours and 2 minutes in 2020, breaking the previous record by more than 7 days. Jamie Aarons broke this record in June 2023, completing the challenge in 31 days, 10 hours and 27 minutes – she almost halved the previous female record time set by Libby Kerr and Lisa Trollope in 2017. A female veteran relay was also completed over 26 days in 2022.

A round of the Munros has no official start or finish and leaves room for individuals to plan a route that suits them. However, the Munros can be grouped into different regions within which mountains can be climbed together with greater logistical ease; for example, Mull, Glenfinnan and the South West Highlands, the Southern Highlands, the Cairngorms, the Central Highlands, the Western Highlands, the Cuillins and the North West Highlands. These areas are further broken down into multiple, smaller peak-bagging rounds, which are excellent challenges in their own right. For example, you can tick off 12 Munros in one push via the Loch Mullardoch Round (see page 112). A continuous Munro Round is a significant undertaking and is a huge challenge for even the fittest of runners and hikers.

The current 24-hour Munro records were both set in 2021: (F) Jasmin Paris bagged 29 Munros and (M) Kim Collison got 33.

WHAT NEXT? If you've already bagged all the Munros then it is probably time to start collecting Corbetts, Marilyns, Grahams, Donalds, Nuttalls, Wainwrights and Birketts!

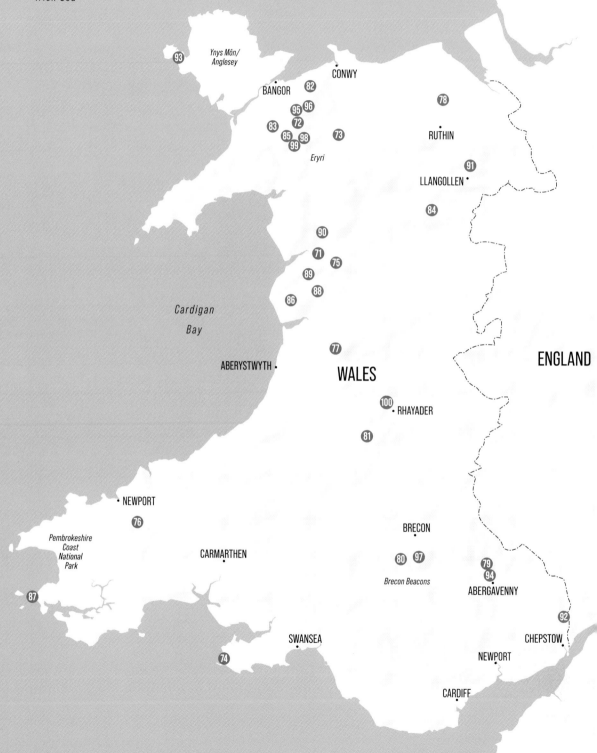

WALES

71 **Dolgellau Parkrun**
5km | TRAIL | NAVIGATION **1**

72 **Llyn Idwal**
4km | TRAIL | NAVIGATION **1**

73 **Llyn Elsi**
6km | TRAIL | NAVIGATION **1**

74 **Rhossili Ranger Run**
10km | TRAIL | NAVIGATION **2**

75 **Waun-oer**
8km | FELL | NAVIGATION **3**

76 **Golden Road**
10km | TRAIL | NAVIGATION **2**

77 **Pen Pumlumon Fawr**
9km | FELL | NAVIGATION **3**

78 **Penycloddiau and
Moel Arthur Hillforts**
12km | TRAIL | NAVIGATION **3**

79 **Sugar Loaf**
11km | FELL | NAVIGATION **3**

80 **Pen y Fan**
9km | TRAIL | NAVIGATION **3**

81 **Drygarn Fawr**
13km | FELL | NAVIGATION **4**

82 **Drum**
13km | TRAIL | NAVIGATION **4**

83 **Moel Eilio**
14km | FELL | NAVIGATION **4**

84 **Berwyn Hills**
14km | FELL | NAVIGATION **4**

85 **Yr Wyddfa/Snowdon Horseshoe**
12km | MOUNTAIN | NAVIGATION **4**

86 **Race the Train**
23km | TRAIL | NAVIGATION **1**

87 **Marloes and Martin's Haven**
11km | TRAIL | NAVIGATION **2**

88 **Corris to Abergynolwyn**
17km | FELL | NAVIGATION **4**

89 **Cadair Idris**
16km | FELL | NAVIGATION **4**

90 **Coed-y-Brenin Half Marathon**
22km | TRAIL | NAVIGATION **1**

91 **Llangollen Fell Race**
27km | FELL | NAVIGATION **1**

92 **Sedbury Cliffs to Monmouth**
29km | TRAIL | NAVIGATION **1**

93 **Ynys Gybi (Holy Island)**
43km | TRAIL | NAVIGATION **1**

94 **Abergavenny Three Peaks**
33km | FELL | NAVIGATION **3**

95 **Welsh 1000m Peaks Race**
33km | MOUNTAIN | NAVIGATION **4**

96 **Welsh 3000s**
38km | MOUNTAIN | NAVIGATION **4**

97 **South Wales Traverse**
117km | FELL | NAVIGATION **4**

98 **Llwybr Llechi Eryri/
Snowdonia Slate Trail**
134km | TRAIL | NAVIGATION **1**

99 **Paddy Buckley Round**
104km | FELL | NAVIGATION **4**

100 **Cambrian Way**
479km | FELL | NAVIGATION **2**

71

DOLGELLAU PARKRUN

5km | **TRAIL** | **NAVIGATION** 1 fully waymarked
GWYNEDD

Easy trails along the Afon Wnion as it flows
towards the beautiful Mawddach Estuary.

DISTANCE **5km** ASCENT **20m** TIME **0:18–0:35 hours**
RECORDS **0:17.43 (F) and 0:15.25 (M)** START/FINISH **Marian Mawr
car park, Dolgellau** GRID REF **SH 727 179** GPS **52.7443, -3.8862**
PUBLIC TRANSPORT **Good bus links in all directions, www.traveline.
cymru** PARKING **Marian Mawr car park (parking charges apply)**
MORE INFO **No dogs are allowed at this parkrun event**

Dolgellau is a convenient base from which to explore
both the mountains and the coast of Eryri (Snowdonia)
National Park. As a former county town, Dolgellau has
a rich history – the bridge over the Afon Wnion dates
back to 1638.

The parkrun course here has two laps of an
out-and-back loop along an old railway line – the
Mawddach Trail. It is run entirely on hard-packed
trails which are shared with other users, including
cyclists and dog walkers.

Starting from the car park, the course is flat and
heads first towards the coast, crossing the footbridge
and turning back just after a picnic bench – there will
be cones and a marshal to give directions on the day
of the event. Run back to the car park, before repeating
the course. The finish is back in the car park area.

72

LLYN IDWAL

4km | **TRAIL** | **NAVIGATION** 1 fully waymarked
ERYRI/ SNOWDONIA

A lakeside loop surrounded by dramatic
mountainous scenery, set within the heart
of Wales's oldest National Nature Reserve.

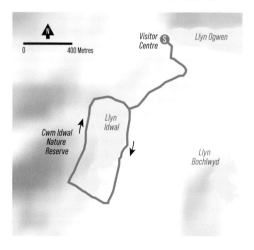

DISTANCE **4km** ASCENT **130m** TIME **0:20–1:00 hours**
START/FINISH **Ogwen Cottage outdoor education centre, Gwynedd**
GRID REF **SH 650 603** GPS **53.1233, -4.0188** PUBLIC TRANSPORT
Sherpa'r Wyddfa buses stop at Llyn Ogwen, www.sherparwyddfa.wales
PARKING **Ogwen Centre car park (parking charges apply) – limited
spaces. Some lay-bys on the A5 – please park considerately**

In this challenge you can get up close and personal
with the ominously named black hole of Twll Du –
widely known as the Devil's Kitchen. This dark, craggy
gully dramatically splits the cliff of Clogwyn y Geifr
at the back of Cwm Idwal, within which there lies a
beautiful lake, surrounded by a fabulous short trail.

A well-made stone path leads up from Ogwen
Cottage to an iron gate on the shore of Llyn Idwal.
The path continues along the shoreline to the southern
end of the lake, where there are two options, the lower
path that sticks to the shore, or a higher, rockier trail
on which you'll climb steep stone steps amid large
glacier-deposited boulders and scree towards the
Devil's Kitchen before descending rocky shelves back
to the shoreline and 'beach' of the lake. (Higher trail:
4.8 kilometres; 190 metres ascent.)

OTHER OPTIONS Other local gems include the Precipice Walk and the Mawddach Trail, which follows the estuary to Barmouth on the coast (there's a longer, more mountainous Mawddach Way too). Coed y Brenin Forest Park is also nearby.

RACE For more information or to register: *www.parkrun. org.uk/dolgellau*

WHAT NEXT? For other Welsh parkruns with trail sections try Colby, Erddig, Grangemoor or Llanerchaeron. For a similar length route but with more off-road and ascent try the Sarn Helen short route in Coed y Brenin Forest Park or the Llyn Elsi trail in Betws-y-Coed (see page 122). You might also enjoy waymarked trail runs at Bwlch nant yr Arian near Aberystwyth; Newborough Forest on Ynys Môn (Anglesey); Tan y Coed near Machynlleth; or the Spirit of Llynfi Woodland near Maesteg.

© SHUTTERSTOCK/ANDREW CHISHOLM

OTHER OPTIONS To extend the challenge, climb Y Garn from the north-west tip of Llyn Idwal. It is only 2 kilometres to the summit from here but involves 540 metres of climbing. The view from the top is a real prize though!

RACE This scenic trail is briefly intercepted by the Ultra-Trail Snowdonia (103- and 168-kilometre races) and overlooked by the Welsh 1000m Peaks Race (see page 154) and day one of the Dragon's Back Race, *www.dragonsbackrace.com*

WHAT NEXT? Try the Llyn Ogwen circular trail from the same start location. Alternatively try the longer run up to Glaslyn beneath Yr Wyddfa (Snowdon) from

Pen-y-Pass (take the Miners' Track up and the Pyg Track back down). Elsewhere in Britain, similar trails include the Hidden Valley of Glencoe; Coire Làgan on the Isle of Skye; Corrie Fee in the Caringorms; the Birks of Aberfeldy in Perth and Kinross; Skelwith, Aria and Colwith forces or Easdale Tarn in the Lake District; the Lizard Point Loop in Cornwall; Lydford Gorge in Devon; or Rhaeadr Ddu Falls in Eryri.

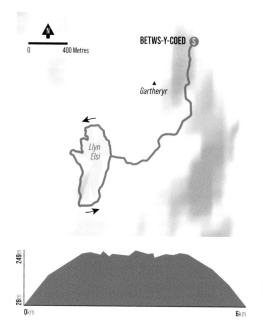

BETWS-Y-COED Ⓢ

Gartheryr

Llyn Elsi

0   400 Metres

249m
28m
0km   6km

73

LLYN ELSI

6km | **TRAIL** | **NAVIGATION 1** fully waymarked
ERYRI/SNOWDONIA

A popular trail through woodland to the
quiet heights of Llyn Elsi, with good views
towards the Carneddau and Glyderau.

DISTANCE **6km** ASCENT **230m** TIME **0:45–1:30 hours**
START/FINISH **St Mary's Church, Betws-y-Coed** GRID REF **SH 794 564**
GPS **53.0912, -3.8023** PUBLIC TRANSPORT **Good bus links across Wales.
To visit by train, travel to Llandudno Junction and then take the
smaller Conwy Valley railway to Betws-y-Coed** PARKING **Multiple car
parks (parking charges apply) within Betws-y-Coed – including on
nearby Station Road**

74

RHOSSILI RANGER RUN

10km | **TRAIL** | **NAVIGATION 2** partial waymarking
GOWER

A rewarding trail run following the Wales
Coast Path alongside Rhossili Down, on to
beautiful shoreline and looping out towards
the shapely Pen Pyrod (Worms Head).

DISTANCE **10km** ASCENT **140m** TIME **1:00–1:30 hours**
START/FINISH **Rhossili car park** GRID REF **SS 414 880**
GPS **51.5685, -4.2897** PUBLIC TRANSPORT There are regular bus
services from Swansea to Rhossili PARKING **Rhossili car park (National
Trust; parking charges apply) – be aware that this car park can get
very busy and can fill in peak season** MORE INFO **Search 'Rhossili
Ranger Run' on www.nationaltrust.org.uk**

The trail starts in Rhossili and follows the waymarked
Wales Coast Path on a good track heading north – a
beautiful stretch of classic, coastal path to savour. When
you reach the buildings of Hillend, descend to the beach
and leave the coast path, turning south along Rhossili
Beach. From here you can enjoy running across the
smooth sand until it's time to climb back up the steep
path to Rhossili village, which will challenge tired legs.
Don't be tempted to stop when you reach the car park
or you'll miss the highlight of running out towards the
intriguing Pen Pyrod (Worms Head). A fantastic clifftop track leads towards the wonderful Lookout Station
viewpoint before you return to Rhossili.

GOOD TO KNOW If you want to explore Pen Pyrod beyond
the Lookout Station make sure you check the tide times
(they are displayed on a board near the causeway)
– the promontory is only accessible for around two
hours either side of low tide. Gower was the first place
in Britain to be named an Area of Outstanding Natural
Beauty (it is now a National Landscape) and the
beaches here have since won many awards.

Charming Betws-y-Coed is a popular village base and is surrounded by Gwydir Forest Park – which offers tons of great low-level running routes. This route encircles the idyllic mountain lake of Llyn Elsi, which supplies the village with water. The lake circuit is on an undulating, well-surfaced path and track, with some boardwalk; it is waymarked with wooden posts/white arrows throughout.

The route passes St Mary's Church, which replaced the 14th-century 'prayer house in the woods' which gives Betws-y-Coed its name. The yew trees here are around 500 years old.

OTHER OPTIONS A number of other waymarked trails within the Gwydir Forest Park start from the Pont-y-Pair car park in the centre of Betws-y-Coed. Both Pen yr Allt and Llyn Parc trails are slightly longer than the Llyn Elsi trail. There are also a number of permanent orienteering courses locally.

RACE The Betws-y-Coed Trail Challenge offers 10K and 5K events on the Llyn Elsi trails. For more information or to enter, visit *www.trailbetws.com*

WHAT NEXT? At Bwlch Nant yr Arian, near Aberystwyth, try the waymarked Y Llo trail (5 kilometres; 90 metres ascent) with views across the Cambrian coastline. The Llyn Idwal circuit (see page 120) is a similar distance with a more mountainous feel. Other lakeside trails worth visiting in Great Britain include the Buttermere loop in the Lake District; Loch Coruisk on the Isle of Skye (see page 59); Loch Ossian on the edge of Rannoch Moor; Loch an Eilein in the Cairngorms (see page 57); Kielder Water in Northumberland; or Malham Tarn in the Yorkshire Dales.

OTHER OPTIONS For something more strenuous in the same area, take a look at the Gower Super Challenge (61 kilometres with 1,230 metres of ascent). This can be split into two shorter day-length runs; Crofty to Rhossili and Rhossili to Bishopston.

RACE Events that visit the Rhossili coastline include the Gower Half Marathon, Marathon and Ultra events from Endurancelife (starting from Oxwich Bay), *www.endurancelife.com/gower* There are also the Gower Coastal Trail Races (Ultra 50, Ultra Bach and Trail Race) by Run Walk Crawl, *www.runwalkcrawl.co.uk*

WHAT NEXT?
For other coastal routes try the Y Gogarth (Great Orme) in North Wales or a coastal path route from Abersoch on the Llŷn Peninsula. Fantastic scenery abounds on many sections of the Isle of Anglesey Coastal Path, the Pembrokeshire Coast Path and the longer South West Coast Path.

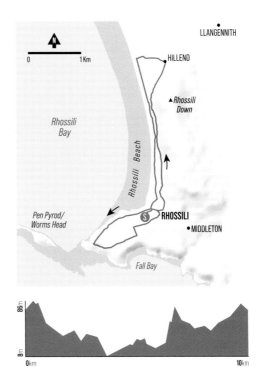

75
WAUN-OER

8km | FELL | NAVIGATION 3 no waymarking
ERYRI/SNOWDONIA

A short, sharp taster of the rugged Meirionnydd Round in the Dyfi Hills, part of the quiet, southern part of Eryri.

DISTANCE **8km** ASCENT **450m** TIME **0:50–1:45 hours**
START **Bwlch Oerddrws, A470** FINISH **Bwlch Llyn Bach, A487**
GRID REF **SH 802 170/SH 753 135** GPS **52.7376, -3.7755/52.7047, -3.8470**
PUBLIC TRANSPORT **Regular buses run from Dolgellau past the start and finish, www.lloydscoaches.com Most buses operate a 'hail and ride' service in rural areas and can stop where it is safe to do so**
PARKING **Roadside car parks at the start and finish (free)**

The Dyfi Hills, in the southern part of Eryri, may be modest in stature when compared with the more dramatic mountains of the north, but runners who choose to explore these quiet hills will be richly rewarded with solitude, expanses of wild moorland, secluded green valleys and open mountain vistas.

The route follows a ridgeline, passing old quarry workings, and heading up to the uneven grassy summit of Waun-oer, which offers fantastic views north to the rest of Eryri. From here you continue to trace the shapely skyline of the Dyfi Hills along to Mynydd Ceiswyn. After you've crossed a minor road, it is best to enter the old quarry on the opposite side, and turn left to pass through a disused area, exiting over a fence to a sloping field, then traverse across the

76
GOLDEN ROAD

10km | TRAIL | NAVIGATION 2 partial waymarking
PEMBROKESHIRE

Run the grassy spine of the Mynydd Preseli (Preseli Hills) – a historically rich traverse known as the Golden Road.

DISTANCE **10km** ASCENT **320m** TIME **1–2 hours** START **Lay-by near Blaenbanon, just off the A478** FINISH **Bwlch-gwynt** GRID REF **SN 165 331/SN 075 322** GPS **51.9660, -4.6724/51.9548, -4.8028**
PUBLIC TRANSPORT **No practical options** PARKING **Roadside car parks/ lay-bys at the start and finish (free)**

field to pick up a good trail making its way down to the finishing car park on the A487.

OTHER OPTIONS An alternative route would be to head east from Cribin Fawr to the summit of Maesglase, then descend around Foel Dinas to meet the A470 6 kilometres further east of the start point, at Dinas Mawddwy.

To extend the route, continue the Meirionnydd Round route west over the Cadair Idris range to Barmouth.

ULTRA ROUTE The Meirionnydd Round is an ultra-distance fell running challenge which weaves its way through rough and remote mountainous terrain including Cadair Idris, the Rhinogydd, Migneint, Arenig and Aran summits as well as the Dyfi Forest (127 kilometres with 6,100 metres of ascent). It was devised and first completed by Yiannis Tridimas in the 1990s. There are plenty of opportunities to meet support runners en route at one of the road crossings, and it logically divides into five legs. The round can be started at any point and completed in either direction. Excellent navigational skills are a must!

RACE Ras Rhobell Fawr and Ras yr Aran (to the summit of Aran Fawddwy) are fell running events in the surrounding hills. For more information or to enter: *www.run-meirionnydd.co.uk*

© HUW GILBERT

WHAT NEXT? Other great runs in the local area include Rhobell Fawr from Llanfachreth, or Arenig Fawr from the south side of Llyn Celyn. Similar examples of short fell routes in Wales include Cnicht, Moel Famau, Moel Siabod or Cribyn. In the Lake District try High Street, Loughrigg Fell, Wansfell and so many more! In Scotland there is Meall a' Bhuachaille (see page 68), Clachnaben, Beinn Resipol or Schiehallion.

The Golden Road is the name given to the trail which traverses Mynydd Preseli (Preseli Hills), with rocky tors, cairns and ancient monuments which date back to Neolithic times. Close to Carn Bica is an eye-shaped ring of stones known as Beddarthur, said to be the last resting place of King Arthur. Note also the jagged shape of Carn Menyn; this is due to the harsh weather eroding the bluestone or dolerite rock from which it is made. The route passes two quarries that are believed to be the source of the famous bluestones, which were used to build Stonehenge over 4,000 years ago.

Despite the steepness, a diversion from the main trail to take in Foeldrygarn is worth the effort for the fabulous view and the chance to see the remains of a substantial Iron Age hillfort. The trio of cairns within are older than the fort and give the hill its name – 'Three Cairns Hill'.

OTHER OPTIONS Why not bag Foel Cwmcerwyn – the highest point in Pembrokeshire – as an out-and-back along the way. To extend further, run this route east

to west and but take the trail heading north at Bwlch Pennant (instead of continuing to the car park at Bwlch-gwynt). This adds in part of the Foel Eryr circular walk, which links trails and a minor road then finishes with a climb up the Foel Eryr viewpoint (468 metres) above the car park on the B4329, *www. pembrokeshirecoast.wales/things-to-do/walking-in-the-park/web-walks/foel-eryr*

RACE The Preseli Beast races offer three different distances – Bach (12 miles), Beast (24 miles) and Ultrabeast (32 miles), *www.preselibeast.com*

WHAT NEXT? For similar routes across Great Britain, check out the Malvern Hills (see page 16); the Carnethy 5 in the Pentland Hills; Bennachie in Aberdeenshire (see page 62); Chrome Hill and Parkhouse Hill in the Peak District; Walla Crag, Angle Tarn or Loughrigg Fell in the Lake District; the Blackdown Hills or the Mendip Hills in the West Country; or Box Hill in Surrey.

© KATE WORTHINGTON

77
PEN PUMLUMON FAWR

9km | FELL | NAVIGATION 3 no waymarking
CAMBRIAN MOUNTAINS

Climb proud Pen Pumlumon Fawr, the most
prominent peak between Cadair Idris in Eryri
and Pen y Fan in the Brecon Beacons.

DISTANCE **9km**   ASCENT **450m**   TIME TIME **1:15–2:15 hours**
START/FINISH **Road end, eastern shore of Nant-y-moch Reservoir**
GRID REF **SN 774 879**   GPS **52.4752, -3.8064**   PUBLIC TRANSPORT
No practical options   PARKING **Park at the road end on the eastern
shore of Nant-y-moch Reservoir, or in lay-bys along the shore. Please
park responsibly, not in passing places**

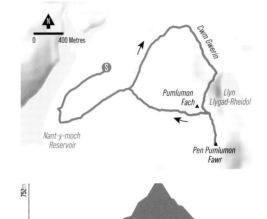

Pen Pumlumon Fawr is the highest point on the
Pumlumon massif (Pumlumon is thought to mean
'Five Tops') and as such is the highest point in the
Cambrian Mountains. It famously holds the sources
of the Afon Hafren (River Severn) and the Afon
Gwy (River Wye), which flow across the border into
England. Climbing Pen Pumlumon Fawr via its less
frequented northern aspect offers runners the best
views over its northern cwm, crags and lakes, and
presents a challenging climb to boot.

Head south from the road end then take the track
leading north-east round the base of the lumpy
Pumlumon Fach and past some small lakes nestled in
a dramatic glacial cwm. A well-used steep trod through
larger boulders and rocky areas grants you an escape on
to the welcome flattening between Pumlumon Fach and
Pen Pumlumon Fawr, with only one final steep ascent to
the summit area. On clear days, there are fantastic views
out to sea and back north to the heights of Eryri.

OTHER OPTIONS Extend this route from Pen Pumlumon
Fawr by heading east to take in the Source of Afon Gwy,

Pen Pumlumon Arwystli and the Source of Afon
Hafren. From here you can drop down the north side
into the valley and follow the Afon Hengwm back to
the reservoir.

RACE Pen Pumlumon Fawr is on the Cambrian Way
(see page 166), and passed on day three of the
Dragon's Back Race.

Alternatively, there is a lower-level 50-kilometre
journey through the Cambrian Mountains called Race
to the Sea (organised by Cambrian Mountain Events).
The route follows the Afon Ystwyth from Llangurig to
Aberystwyth, *www.cambrianevents.co.uk/race-to-the-sea*

WHAT NEXT? For similar fell running routes in Wales try
Drygarn Fawr (see page 130), Moel Eilio (see page 132)
or Cnicht. In the Lake District you might try Wansfell,
Cat Bells and High Spy or the Hay Stacks circular. In
Scotland, the Culter Fell circuit, Meall a' Bhuachaille
(see page 68), The Cobbler, Campsie Fells or the Ochil
Hills – for something a bit bigger and wilder try the
Rois-Bheinn Round from Inverailort.

78
PENYCLODDIAU AND MOEL ARTHUR HILLFORTS

12km | TRAIL | NAVIGATION 3 no waymarking
DENBIGHSHIRE

Visit the ancient hillforts crowning two
prominent summits in the Clwydian Range.

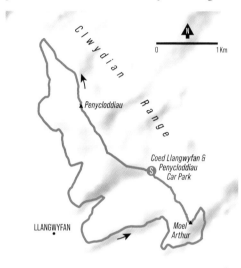

DISTANCE **12km** ASCENT **450m** TIME **1:30–2:15 hours**
START/FINISH **Coed Llangwyfan and Penycloddiau car park** GRID REF
SJ 138 668 GPS **53.1917, -3.2908** PUBLIC TRANSPORT **Local buses from
Denbigh stop in Llangwyfan, which is 3 kilometres from the start**
PARKING **Coed Llangwyfan and Penycloddiau car park (free)**

It's an easy descent on grassy tracks and forest
trail to a road crossing, followed by the ascent to the
rounded top of Moel Arthur – a perfect setting for an
ancient hillfort and a breather! This hillfort is much
smaller than its neighbour, but has vast ramparts and
ditches for its size. Unique limestone tools and Bronze
Age copper axes have been found here. Save some
energy for the final steep descent.

GOOD TO KNOW The high-level section of this run follows
Offa's Dyke Path National Trail, which runs almost the
entire length of the Clwydian Range before heading
into the Dee Valley (see page 148 for a run on another
part of Offa's Dyke Path).

OTHER OPTIONS This route can be extended at both ends
to make a full (linear) traverse of the Clwydian Range.
The Clwydian Tops Challenge is an informal peak bagging mission utilising sections of the Offa's Dyke Path.

RACE Various fell races are held in the Clwydian Hills;
for details or to enter visit *www.clwydianfellrace.org*

WHAT NEXT? In Wales, take a look at Moel Eilio (see page
132), the Mynydd Preseli traverse (see page 124)
and the Berwyn Hills (see page 134). For similar
routes elsewhere, seek out challenges in the Pentland
Hills, Ochil Hills, Cheviots, North York Moors and
neighbouring Cleveland Hills. Why not build up your
base and tackle the longer but super-classic Edale
Skyline (see page 24)!

The Clwydian Range of hills, a National Landscape,
is a chain of windswept and heather-clad summits,
which offers varied trail running and an abundance
of historical remains. Iron Age hillforts dominate
the landscape and the challenge here is to link the
fascinating Penycloddiau and Moel Arthur forts in
a single undulating journey.

Good bridleways and tracks contour across the
hillside to gain Offa's Dyke Path, which leads to
Penycloddiau hillfort. This is the largest hillfort on
the Clwydian Range, and one of the largest in Wales,
encircling a vast area (21 hectares), with multiple
concentric ditches and ramparts, and a three-metre-
wide drystone wall.

79
SUGAR LOAF

11km | **FELL** | **NAVIGATION 3** no waymarking
THE BLACK MOUNTAINS

A classic up-and-down route on one of the most iconic peaks in the Black Mountains.

The Sugar Loaf (Y Fâl) has a striking outline that has led to the popular misconception that it's an extinct volcano. In fact, it is composed entirely of old red sandstone like the rest of the Black Mountains range, but it is nevertheless a much-loved vantage point with panoramic views across the Brecon Beacons.

The climbing starts with a steepening trail through woodland (designated a Site of Special Scientific Interest), which eventually breaks out to head up to the ridge of Deri (Welsh for oak). The second notable ascent is up to the summit of Y Fâl via a well-used track on its higher, steeper slopes. At 596 metres, Y Fâl falls four metres short of attaining 'mountain' status, but you'll still notice the climb!

Take a moment on the busy summit to soak up the expansive views. Numerous trails criss-cross the hillside, but the race route drops steeply off the summit towards the long ridge of Rholben. No sooner have you reached flatter ground (at approximately 400 metres), the trail plunges down again towards woodland to the south-east. Enjoy the descent back to Abergavenny.

OTHER OPTIONS For a longer race in the same area, take a look at the Black Mountains Fell Race from Llanbedr. The high ground of Y Fâl doesn't join directly to other fells, but it is possible to link it to Blorens (Blorenge), and Ysgyryd Fawr (Skirrid) via connecting low-level trails (see the Abergavenny Three Peaks route – page 152).

RACE The standard fell race hasn't run for the last few years, but the route is still a cracker. Race records stood at: (F) J. Hemming with 1:00.10 in 2010; (M) M. Collins with 0:49.09 in 2006. As an alternative, check out the Night Sugar (one of several night fell races across the UK, including the nearby Blorenge Night Roundabout) or Winter Sugar Loaf races.

DISTANCE **11km** ASCENT **590m** TIME **1:15–2:00 hours** START/FINISH **Abergavenny Leisure Centre car park** GRID REF **SO 297 152** GPS **51.8310, -3.0210** PUBLIC TRANSPORT **Good bus and rail links with surrounding towns** PARKING **Car park at the leisure centre (free) or use Fairfield car park nearby (parking charges apply)**

WHAT NEXT? Similar classic fell races include Ras Tarren-hendre (10 kilometres; 610 metres ascent) and Moel Siabod (9 kilometres; 700 metres ascent), both in Eryri. Elsewhere in Great Britain try the Blisco Dash, Latrigg, Glaramara or Steel Fell in the Lake District, or Roseberry Topping or Great Whernside in North Yorkshire.

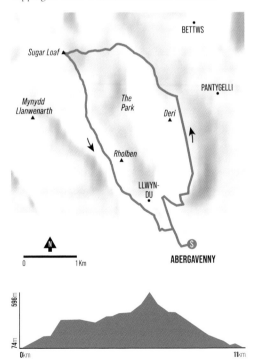

80
PEN Y FAN

9km | TRAIL | NAVIGATION 3 no waymarking
BRECON BEACONS

An easily recognisable and much-loved angular summit in the Brecon Beacons National Park; the highest mountain in southern Britain.

As the highest mountain in the Brecon Beacons National Park, Pen y Fan's popularity rivals even Yr Wyddfa (Snowdon). As you start at 430 metres, this smaller peak is a more accessible objective for anyone looking to dip their toe into mountain running. Once up high, shapely mountains and dramatic connecting ridges soar over open moorland below.

Rather than sticking to the more direct Cambrian Way, this route forks left up Y Gyrn, before swinging round on to the interesting north-west ridge overlooking Llyn Cwm Llwch to reach the rocky summit of Corn Du. There is a precipitous edge on the north side, which accentuates the feeling of exposure. The trail follows the edge closely, dropping north-east to the broader south-west ridge of Pen y Fan. To escape the busy triangular summit, use the lower, contouring

DISTANCE **9km** ASCENT **480m** TIME **1:30–2:30 hours**
START/FINISH **Pont ar Daf car park** GRID REF **SN 986 199**
GPS **51.8692, -3.4727** PUBLIC TRANSPORT **Regular bus service, get off at the Storey Arms, www.traveline.cymru** PARKING **Pont ar Daf car park (parking charges apply)**

trail to Bwlch Duwynt, then head south-west on a well-engineered trail (Taff Trail) which drops directly back to Pont ar Daf car park.

OTHER OPTIONS To cut the route short, simply miss out the summit of Pen y Fan and join the descent route from Corn Du (Granny Path) by heading south from the summit to Bwlch Duwynt. Extend the challenge with a full circular of the major summits (to include Cribyn and Fan y Big), also known as the Brecon Beacons Horseshoe.

Pen y Fan is part of the wider 'Welsh Three Peaks' challenge. This involves ascending Pen y Fan, Cadair Idris and Yr Wyddfa in one continuous journey (usually driving or cycling in between).

RACE For more details on the annual Pen y Fan Race, visit *www.breconfans.org.uk/pen-y-fan-race* This race is part of the Brecon Fans Race Weekend – two great horseshoes on consecutive days!

If you want to race all of the Welsh Three Peaks, then you'll also need to sign up for the Cadair Idris mountain race (Râs y Gader) and Râs Yr Wyddfa.

The 10YFAN challenge event really throws down the gauntlet! How many times can you summit Pen y Fan in 24 hours? *www.10yfan.com*

WHAT NEXT? Try the Fan y Big Horseshoe from Llanfrynach. For similar Welsh summits try Sugar Loaf (see opposite), Moel Famau, Moel Siabod, Fan Brycheiniog, Penybegwn (Hay Bluff) and Twmpa or the more rugged Cadair Idris (see page 144). Across Great Britain, iconic alternatives might include Cat Bells (see page 4) or Skiddaw in the Lake District; Pen y Ghent in the Yorkshire Dales; Mam Tor or Chrome Hill in the Peak District; The Cobbler in the Southern Highlands; the Pap of Glencoe in the Highlands; Stac Pollaidh in Assynt; or Ben Venue in the Trossachs.

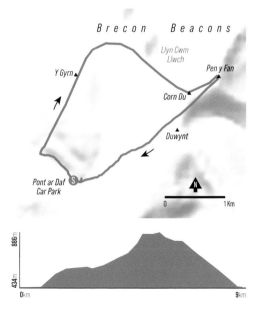

81
DRYGARN FAWR

13km | **FELL** | **NAVIGATION 4** difficult self-navigation or complex terrain
CAMBRIAN MOUNTAINS

Run to the massive cairn that marks the summit of Drygarn Fawr, a stark peak above the Elan Valley in a massif that is littered by Bronze Age cairns and surrounded by wild, tussocky moorland.

DISTANCE **13km** ASCENT **440m** TIME **1:30–3:00 hours**
START/FINISH **South-west corner of Dolymynach Reservoir**
GRID REF **SN 900 616** GPS **52.2418, -3.6113** PUBLIC TRANSPORT
No practical options PARKING **Dolymynach Reservoir car park (free)**
MORE INFO **www.elanvalley.org.uk**

The landscape of the Elan Valley is synonymous with a great many dams and reservoirs – feats of civil engineering that contribute significantly to the area's considerable scenic beauty. The mountains here are rough, lonely peaks that see few hikers and runners compared to the summits of the neighbouring Brecon Beacons and Eryri national parks. Discerning runners will appreciate this valley's rugged beauty, where the vague trods and pathless moorland keep even the most discerning of navigators on their toes.

The route follows the Rhiwnant up the valley, then follows the re-entrant of Nant y Ast up to around 470 metres in height, breaking out south-west over rough and peaty ground directly for Drygarn Fawr's craggy true summit and its large beehive cairn. Note that the flat, upland terrain here can be very exposed in poor weather.

A better trail leads down to Bwylch Trypeg. From here's it's possible to make a short out-and-back to bag the other large ancient cairn on the ridge at Carreg yr Ast. Continue down to the tarn at Bryn Rhudd and yet more collections of stones and cairns at Bwlch y Ddau Faen. The going improves as you descend from here, joining better tracks to meet your outward route again.

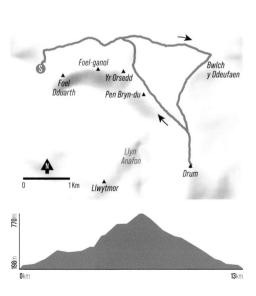

82
DRUM

13km | **TRAIL** | **NAVIGATION 4** difficult self-navigation or complex terrain
ERYRI/SNOWDONIA

As the northern gateway to the Carneddau mountain range, Drum offers steady running on good tracks and views to the coast.

DISTANCE **13km** ASCENT **620m** TIME **1:30–2:45 hours**
START/FINISH **Upper car park, Coedydd Aber National Nature Reserve**
GRID REF **SH 675 716** GPS **53.2249, -3.9849** PUBLIC TRANSPORT
Regular buses run between Bangor and Llandudno, stopping at nearby Abergwyngregyn PARKING **There are two car parks in the nature reserve (parking charges apply) or there is a parking lay-by in Abergwyngregyn (free)**

OTHER OPTIONS The descent route can be extended to include the trig on Gorllwyn and even Y Gamriw. Alternatively, descend south-west after Drygarn Fawr, dropping into the lovely Abergwesyn Valley, for an enjoyable linear run.

RACE Drygarn Fawr is visited on day four of the Dragon's Back Race. There is also the nearby Rhayader Round the Lakes 30K and 10K events, organised by Rhayader Running Club, *www.rhayaderac.org.uk*

WHAT NEXT? For longer challenge in this area try the Reservoir Roundabout Challenge. Starting and finishing at Elan Valley Visitor Centre, this event has two courses – 19 and 34 kilometres in length. Similar fell running can be found on Pen Pumlumon Fawr (see page 126), on Moel Eilio (see page 132) and in Mynydd Preseli (the Preseli Hills – see page 124). Other suggestions include the Great Ridge or Kinder Scout and Kinder Downfall in the Peak District; Blencathra or the Old Man of Coniston in the Lake District; The Cobbler in the Southern Highlands; Merrick (see page 70) and Shalloch on Minnoch in Southern Scotland; or Suilven (see page 88) or Quinag in the North West Highlands.

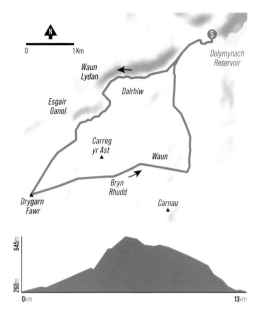

The Carneddau mountain range is the northernmost area of Eryri National Park and constitutes the largest mass of high ground over 3,000 feet in either England or Wales. The sheer scale, gentle gradients and undulating plateaus make this area a fantastic runners' playground.

The route starts on the waymarked North Wales Path, an old Roman road, which contours beneath the foothills of the Carneddau, gently rising towards a crossroads of trails at Bwlch y Ddeufaen. From here a trail heads uphill on to a grassy shoulder leading to the summit of Drum. Drum's summit (over a fence stile) stands at 770 metres and offers fantastic views across the North Wales coast and foothills of the Carneddau.

To descend, follow the track which passes to the north of Pen Bryn-du, winding round the hillside before merging with the North Wales Path again at 400 metres to put you back on the trail back to the start.

OTHER OPTIONS Retreat the way you came if bailing early. A good low-level alternative is the out-and-back trail to Llyn Anafon, which lies beneath the steep western flank of Drum. To extend the adventure, why not continue from Drum over Foel-fras to create a longer horseshoe route which finishes via Rhaeadr-fawr.

The Rhaeadr-fawr waterfall, known locally as Aber Falls, has been popular with tourists since Victorian times and today there is a short trail (waymarked in yellow).

RACE Drum is passed on day one of the Dragon's Back Race.

WHAT NEXT? If you have enjoyed this route in the Carneddau and want something slightly longer, try a round of the northern Carneddau from Cwm Eigiau (Melynllyn Hone Quarry road end parking), the Berwyn Hills (see page 134) or the Brecon Beacons Horseshoe. Elsewhere in Great Britain you might enjoy the Fairfield Horseshoe or the Coledale Horseshoe (see page 18) in the Lake District; or for higher summits, Glen Clova or the White Mounth Munros (see page 89) in the Cairngorms; or the Tyndrum Hills in Loch Lomond and the Trossachs National Park.

83

MOEL EILIO

14km | FELL | NAVIGATION 4 difficult self-navigation
or complex terrain
ERYRI/SNOWDONIA

Runnable and quiet hills above the busy town
of Llanberis, with views to Yr Wyddfa.

> DISTANCE **14km** ASCENT **750m** TIME **1:30–2:45 hours**
> START/FINISH **Llanberis** GRID REF **SH 582 598** GPS **53.1164, -4.1201**
> PUBLIC TRANSPORT **Sherpa'r Wyddfa buses stop at Llanberis,**
> **www.sherparwyddfa.wales** PARKING **Various car parks in Llanberis**
> **(parking charges apply)**

A round of Moel Eilio and its neighbouring peaks is
achievable even when time is short. Flowing running
over grassy summits with fabulous views to Yr
Wyddfa make this the perfect mini challenge away
from the crowds.

The route takes good bridleways and tracks up out
of Llanberis, then breaks off up steep grass and heather
to take a narrow trod which joins the main route up
Moel Eilio from Bwlch-y-groes. Follow the fence line
up Moel Eilio. Enjoy the summit views of Yr Wyddfa,
the Glyderau, the Llŷn Peninsula (known as Snowdon's
Arm) and across to Ynys Môn (Anglesey).

The pleasant grassy ridge leads on over the summits
of Foel Gron and Foel Goch, with wonderful views
across to the Nantlle Ridge, before a steep grassy
slope drops you down to Bwlch Maesgwm. A well-
engineered track leads back down Maesgwm, known
locally as Telegraph Valley due to a past row of poles,
to Llanberis.

OTHER OPTIONS To cut the route short at Moel Eilio,
descend its north ridge, then link trails heading east
via Maen-llwyd-uchaf to join a minor road back to
town. To extend the route, why not continue up to the
summit of Yr Wyddfa!

RACE Ras Moel Eilio is a popular local fell race – it is
actually one of the longest established fell races in
Eryri, being over 40 years old. These hills also form part
of the famous Paddy Buckley Round (see page 164).

WHAT NEXT? If you enjoyed this route, then try a round
in the Moelwynion for something a bit wilder, or

otherwise try trails in the Berwyn Hills (see page
134) or Clwydian Range (see page 127). Elsewhere
try the Sedbergh Hills in Cumbria; the Chevy Chase
in Northumberland (see page 29); or the Pentland
Skyline in Southern Scotland (see page 94).

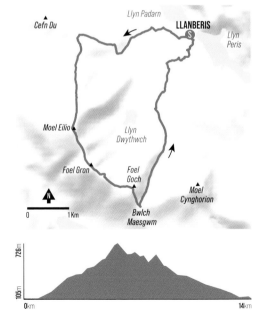

84
BERWYN HILLS

14km | FELL | NAVIGATION 4 difficult self-navigation
or complex terrain
POWYS

Link quiet tops through heather and grass in
a sweeping upland tour of the Berywn Hills.
A great choice for lovers of solitude.

DISTANCE **14km** ASCENT **580m** TIME **2-3 hours** START/FINISH **Lane
next to Tyn-y-ffridd Farm, Cwm Maen Gwynedd** GRID REF **SJ 118 306**
GPS **52.8659, -3.3105** PUBLIC TRANSPORT **No practical options**
PARKING **Small lay-by (room for 2-3 cars). Park considerately – do not
block any gates or farm tracks**

The Berwyn Hills are a high area of sweeping moorland, south of Llangollen. Although mostly heather
and grass, the highest peak of the range, Cadair
Berwyn, is an exception, with its steep and rocky
escarpments. Despite being a lofty 827 metres high,
the summit has very few visitors, and provides an
excellent run when linked with its neighbouring tops.

This circuit takes in Mynydd Tarw and Foel Wen,
then heads west revealing interesting views of Cadair
Berwyn's rocky skyline. The third summit is Tomle and
the final climb of the day is obvious as you follow the
steepening path on to the summit plateau of Cadair
Berwyn and along the escarpment edge to the summit
cairn. There's a short descent on soft ground, but the
route soon rises again to a prominent area of the ridge,
overlooking Llyn Lluncaws.

A path descends through some steep rocks, then on
over Moel yr Ewig to the final summit of Godor. From
here, no public footpaths are marked on maps, but
there is an obviously travelled route from the summit
that heads generally east/south-east towards a well-
used public footpath back to the valley.

OTHER OPTIONS To extend slightly, bag Cadair Bronwen (as an out-and-back) or add a short detour to the summit of Moel Sych before descending to Moel yr Ewig. In these hills, there are many options for continuing to add summits to produce various long, high-level outings. Further north follow the waymarked North Berwyn Way, crossing the range from west to east, between Corwen and Llangollen (25 kilometres; 840 metres ascent).

For a much shorter alternative, simply climb Cadair Berwyn from the south from Tan-y-pistyll – via one of the most spectacular waterfalls in the country!

WHAT NEXT? In Wales try the Llangollen Hills, Moel Eilio (see page 132), the Preseli Hills (see page 124) or the Clwydian Range (see page 127). For similar routes elsewhere, seek out challenges in the Pentland Hills, Ochil Hills, Cheviots, North York Moors or the neighbouring Cleveland Hills. Take it to the next level with the Edale Skyline (see page 24).

85

YR WYDDFA/SNOWDON HORSESHOE

12km | MOUNTAIN | NAVIGATION 4 difficult self-navigation or complex terrain
ERYRI/SNOWDONIA

Link the narrow ridges of Crib Goch and Y Lliwedd via the highest point in Wales and circumnavigate Yr Wyddfa's massive eastern cwm.

DISTANCE **12km** ASCENT **860m** TIME **2–4 hours**
RECORDS **(F)** Sarah Ridgway 1:43.20 in 2011; **(M)** Finlay Wild 1:20.16 in 2019 START/FINISH **Pen-y-Pass** GRID REF **SH 647 556** GPS **53.0804, -4.0213** PUBLIC TRANSPORT Sherpa'r Wyddfa buses stop at Pen-y-Pass, www.sherparwyddfa.wales PARKING Pen-y-Pass car park (parking charges apply) operates a pre-booking system in high season – it is very busy and often full. Alternatives include a parking lay-by near Llyn Pen-y-Gwryd (parking charges apply) or Nant Peris Park and Ride

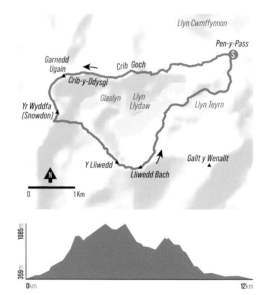

The Yr Wyddfa Horseshoe is a long-standing British mountaineering classic which has gradually succumbed to the fast-and-light approach of fell runners and more recently sky runners. It is the ultimate technical sky run in Eryri National Park. The FKT was taken by Finlay Wild in 2019, who broke local hardman Gareth Wyn Hughes' marker by 3 minutes.

Starting from Pen-y-Pass, you head up to Crib Goch, which is an exhilarating and airy grade-1 ridge scramble (it is exposed, with few options for escape), culminating in the three famous pinnacles, the last of which it is necessary to tackle head-on, going 'up and over'. As you approach the top of the ridge, the scrambly Crib-y-Ddysgl ridge lies ahead and after this exposed section there are several false tops leading to a trig point on the summit of Garnedd Ugain (the second highest peak in Wales at 1,065 metres).

You'll have to join the crowds heading along to the summit of Yr Wyddfa for a while, but can soon escape down the Watkin Path, then over the rocky spine of Y Lliwedd and over multiple small peaks, before dropping down to an easier path back to Pen-y-Pass. Behind you, you can see the entirety of the horseshoe and revel in the glory of what you have just accomplished.

GOOD TO KNOW For the best experience, start early to avoid the crowds. Be careful in high winds; Crib Goch is a notorious accident blackspot.

In winter the ridges on this route are serious mountaineering endeavours and should not be undertaken without the appropriate skills and equipment.

OTHER OPTIONS The only feasible escape route from Crib Goch is from Bwlch Coch (descend to the north or south with extreme care). The second half of the route can be eliminated by descending the comparatively easy Pyg Track or Miners' Track back to Pen-y-Pass.

RACE The terrain on this challenge forms part of the longer Snowdon Skyrace, which traverses both sides of the Snowdon Horseshoe, as well as the north ridge of Tryfan (38 kilometres; 3,470 metres of ascent), *www.apexrunning.co* The horseshoe is also run with a different finishing section on day one of the infamous Dragon's Back Race.

WHAT NEXT? Mountain running routes with a similar character include the Ben Nevis Horseshoe, the Helvellyn Edges (see page 11) or the Ring of Steall (see page 82). For routes that link more difficult sections of graded scrambling, consider the Clach Glas–Bla Bheinn traverse on Skye or the longer Round of Glencoe.

86
RACE THE TRAIN

23km | **TRAIL** | **NAVIGATION** **1** *fully waymarked*
ERYRI/SNOWDONIA

Race your heart out cross-country, along the line of the historic Talyllyn Railway, and beat that train!

DISTANCE **approximately 23km**   ASCENT **approximately 460m**
TIME **2–3 hours**   START/FINISH **Tywyn Wharf station**   GRID REF **SH 585 004**
GPS **52.5837, -4.0892**   PUBLIC TRANSPORT **Tywyn mainline railway station is a short walk from the start. Tywyn also has good bus links with surrounding towns and villages**   PARKING **There is a car park adjacent to the Wharf station. Note that on race day there will be a one-way system in operation and a diversion around road closures**

This unique and acclaimed race, known as the Rotary Challenge, was conceived by local dentist Godfrey Worsey and was first run in 1984. The aim of the challenge is to race along the line of the Talyllyn narrow-gauge steam railway from Tywyn to Abergynolwyn and back. It is the first preserved railway in the world and is one of the Great Little Trains of Wales.

Runners will cross a mixture of public roads, lanes, unmetalled roads, tracks, agricultural land and rough grazing pastures – much of which is private land and very muddy! On race day the route is well signed, running along both sides of the railway line at various points. While some elite runners stay ahead of the train for the full distance, the train stops in various locations to take on water and pass other trains. It also has to turn around at Abergynolwyn. These delays and handicaps allow other runners to overtake the train and add to the uncertainty of the outcome!

BOTH PHOTOS © BARBARA FULLER

GOOD TO KNOW The challenge is predominantly on private land and **must not be run at any other time**. Failure to comply with this request could result in cancellation of future events.

OTHER OPTIONS As well as the 23-kilometre Rotary Challenge, there are four other challenge events on the same day (they are all 10 kilometres or less; some are suitable for children): the Quarry Challenge, the Dolgoch Challenge, the Tynllwynhen Challenge and the Toddlers Trot.

RACE For details of the event and to enter, visit *www.racethetrain.com*

WHAT NEXT? If you're looking for another equally strange but captivating race in Wales, check out the historic Man versus Horse race in Llanwrtyd Wells (35 kilometres), where runners compete against riders on horseback!

87

MARLOES AND MARTIN'S HAVEN

11km | TRAIL | NAVIGATION 2 partial waymarking
PEMBROKESHIRE

Run the cliff edge on this stunning section of the Pembrokeshire Coast Path on the Marloes Peninsula.

DISTANCE **11km** ASCENT **260m** TIME **1:15–1:45 hours**
START/FINISH **Marloes Sands National Trust car park** GRID REF
SM 779 082 GPS **51.7286, -5.2170** PUBLIC TRANSPORT **No practical
options** PARKING **Marloes Sands National Trust car park (parking
charges apply)** MORE INFO **www.nationaltrust.org.uk/visit/wales/
marloes-sands-and-mere**

Starting west of Marloes village, this route first heads south to meet the coastline at Marloes Sands. Heading west on the coast path you'll pass Gateholm Island, the site of a prehistoric settlement – if you're there at low tide you can cross to the island and explore. Further out to sea are the larger islands of Skokholm and Skomer.

Further round the coast the route briefly leaves the Wales Coast Path for a loop around the Deer Park –

the area at the far end of the peninsula. You won't see any deer (the area is named due to a failed attempt to set up a deer park in the 19th century), but you might see Welsh mountain ponies or seals.

Back on the Pembrokeshire Coast Path, continue round to Musselwick Sands, a gorgeous stretch of golden sand which is covered by the sea at high tide, then follow paths and quiet roads back to the start.

OTHER OPTIONS To extend the challenge, simply tackle connecting sections of the coast path. One option is to continue south to St Ann's Head and cut back through Dale village. For more information on planning, visit *www.pembrokeshirecoast.wales/coast-path*

ULTRA ROUTE The full Pembrokeshire Coast Path is a 299-kilometre journey almost entirely within the Pembrokeshire Coast National Park, linking precipitous cliffs, secret coves, wide beaches and sweeping estuaries. If you complete the full distance, you can claim your certificate from the National Park Authority, *www.pembrokeshirecoast.wales*

RACE Endurancelife runs 10K, half marathon, marathon and ultra races on the Pembrokeshire Coast Path, *www.endurancelife.com/pembrokeshire*

WHAT NEXT? The Gower Coast Path is also stunning and, further north, the Llŷn Peninsula offers somewhat wilder coastal trails. Elsewhere in Great Britain, check out coastal sections of the South Downs Way and also the South West Coast Path – notably the Jurassic Coast for its dramatic beauty, and the North Cornwall and North Devon coastlines for a wild, more rugged feel.

88
CORRIS TO ABERGYNOLWYN

17km | **FELL** | **NAVIGATION 4** difficult self-navigation or complex terrain
ERYRI/SNOWDONIA

A peaceful section of the Corris Round, a long mountain journey created by a 12-year-old resident of Corris.

DISTANCE **17km** ASCENT **860m** TIME **2:00–3:30 hours** START **Corris**
FINISH **Abergynolwyn** GRID REF **SH 754 078/SH 677 069**
GPS **52.6535, -3.8433/52.6436, -3.9567** PUBLIC TRANSPORT **Local buses connect Corris and Abergynolwyn with surrounding towns and villages, www.lloydscoaches.com** PARKING **On-street parking available in Corris and Abergynolwyn. Park considerately**
MORE INFO **Watch the film about Tom's challenge by Rob Johnson: www.filmuphigh.com/the-corris-round**

During the Coronavirus lockdown of 2020, exercise was restricted to once a day and on routes 'from home' to help prevent the spread of the virus. This brought about a flurry of locally inspired rounds and challenges, many of which gained popularity after lockdown ended. The Corris Round is one such route; it was created by 12-year-old Tom Gilbert, who lives in Corris. This challenge is the first logical section of Tom's route.

From Corris, a path zigzags steeply up through forestry, before meeting more engineered forest tracks overlooking the village. Mountain bike tracks from Dyfi Bike Park aid progress towards the ridgeline, which rises to the summit of Tarren y Gesail (which is approached from the opposite side on day three of the Dragon's Back Race). A steep, grassy trail leads southeast back into the forest, then west along an undulating ridge towards the grassy ascent to Tarrenhendre. Steep grass leads down to zigzagging forest tracks and on to Nant Gwernol and along the riverside path to the village of Abergynolwyn.

© HUW GILBERT

OTHER OPTIONS There are numerous points where it is possible to drop off the ridgeline and link up trails and forestry tracks to reach the nearest road (but there are no roads very close by). Between Foel y Geifr and Pant Gwyn there are trails that drop north/north-west towards the old Bryn-Eglwys Quarry, cutting out the final section over Tarrenhendre.

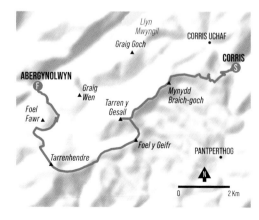

ULTRA ROUTE The full Corris Round is a roller-coaster run over 12 local Hewitts, with a distance of 49 kilometres and 3,170 metres of ascent. Tom and his dad, Huw, completed it in 11 hours and 28 minutes.

RACE Ras Tarrenhendre is a short local fell race (10 kilometres; 610 metres ascent) organised by Meirionnydd Running Club which traces a loop from Abergynolwyn over Tarrenhendre summit, *www.run-meirionnydd.co.uk*

WHAT NEXT? Sections of the Meirionnydd Round (see page 124) or the Paddy Buckley Round (see page 164) would be the logical next step up from this route, building towards a full leg or eventually a whole round. Similar rounds include the Bay Limestone Round, which takes in 13 summits around Morecambe Bay (see page 44); or George Fisher's Tea Round (see page 38) or the Cumbrian Traverse (see page 42) in the Lake District.

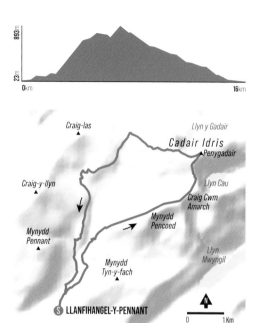

89
CADAIR IDRIS

16km | FELL | NAVIGATION 4 difficult self-navigation or complex terrain
ERYRI/SNOWDONIA

A magnificent mountain massif, with dramatic cwms, glacial lakes and shoulders radiating down to Dolgellau and the coast above Barmouth.

DISTANCE **16km** ASCENT **890m** TIME **2:30–4:00 hours** START/FINISH **Llanfihangel-y-pennant** GRID REF **SH 671 088** GPS **52.6605, -3.9664** PUBLIC TRANSPORT **Llanfihangel-y-pennant is 3km north of Abergynolwyn, which has good bus links with surrounding towns and villages, www.lloydscoaches.com** PARKING **Small parking area opposite the church in Llanfihangel-y-pennant (free)**

90
COED-Y-BRENIN HALF MARATHON

22km | TRAIL | NAVIGATION 1 fully waymarked
ERYRI/SNOWDONIA

Hop roots, mud and rocks on this varied route, linking forest roads and rough trails from the award-winning Coed-y-Brenin visitor centre.

DISTANCE **22km** ASCENT **610m** TIME **2:45–3:45 hours** RECORDS **(F) Emma Clayton 1:36.36 in 2018; (M) Andrew Davis 1:21.41 in 2015** START/FINISH **Coed-y-Brenin visitor centre** GRID REF **SH 723 268** GPS **52.8243, -3.8962** PUBLIC TRANSPORT **Bus services from Dolgellau and Blaenau Ffestiniog will stop by request at the entrance road to the visitor centre on the A470** PARKING **Coed-y-Brenin visitor centre car park (parking charges apply)** MORE INFO **www.naturalresources. wales/days-out/places-to-visit/north-west-wales/coed-y-brenin-visitor-centre**

Coed-y-Brenin Forest is not only popular with mountain bikers, it has five waymarked running trails too. In 2022, the forest hosted the opening round of the inaugural Salomon UK Golden Trail National Series, *www.goldentrailseries.com/races/trail-marathon-wales-34.htm*

The half marathon trail is waymarked by a green arrow and delivers fantastic undulating running over the Cefndeuddwr ridge, along the Afon Mawddach, past Mynydd Bâch and down to Afon Wen. Then the sting in the tail – a steep climb back over the Cefndeuddwr ridge, before an easier-angled descent to the visitor centre to finish. Look out for unexpected views of the mountains of southern Eryri as the forest opens up at various points along the way.

OTHER OPTIONS For shorter options in the forest park, try the Goldrush (waymarked in orange – 14 kilometres), the Sarn Helen Long (waymarked in blue – eight kilometres) or the Sarn Helen Short (waymarked in yellow – five kilometres). Follow the waymarkers or pick up a running trails leaflet from the visitor centre. The full marathon (race route – only waymarked on race day)

Cadair Idris; Cader Idris; Penygadair; or, indeed, Pen y Gader! There is an array of titles for this majestic peak, which rises stupendously from the lowlands of the Afon Mawddach to the north, and the Dyfi Forest to the south-east. Local folklore describes Idris as a giant who lived on this mountain (Cadair Idris is Welsh for 'Idris's Chair') and it is said that if you survive a night on 'the chair', the ordeal will either drive you mad or turn you into a poet! This challenge allows runners to top out on the mountain's highest point via Mynydd Pencoed, a broad, grassy shoulder rising above Llanfihangel-y-pennant.

The trail contours above fields before making a steep uphill effort towards the summit of Mynydd Pencoed. The route then follows the rising ridgeline towards the dramatic edge of Craig Cau, above the glacial lake of Llyn Cau below, said to be the prison of a water dragon trapped there by King Arthur. Above, a well-used mountain path climbs to the rocky summit of Cadair Idris. To descend, take the Pony Path down through rocky channels, hugging the edge of the steep cwm above Llyn y Gadair, then follow a well-trodden bridleway that weaves its way down through open fields towards the valley.

OTHER OPTIONS There are several different routes up Cadair Idris; the Minffordd Path and the Pony Path are the most popular. Note that although the Fox's Path from Llyn Gwernan is the most direct and shortest route, a good portion of it is on scree and it is very steep at the top – use with caution.

RACE If you want to race over Cadair Idris then sign up for the Ras y Gader (17 kilometres with 920 metres of ascent), an event that starts and finishes in the market town of Dolgellau. The race is a popular classic that often sells out; the course records are (F) 1:33.58 and (M) 1:21.18. For more details or to enter, visit *www.cader-race.co.uk*

WHAT NEXT? Why not complete the Welsh Three Peaks and climb Pen y Fan and Yr Wyddfa too (see pages 129 and 136). Other remarkable hills of a similar stature include Blencathra and the Old Man of Coniston in the Lake District or Buachaille Etive Mòr in Glen Coe. For something with a wilder feel try Slioch, a Munro in Wester Ross, or Ben More on the Isle of Mull.

---

uses trails on both sides of the A470, *www.runcyb.com/trail-marathon-wales*

RACE The Salomon Trail Marathon Wales event takes place here, as do a number of other trail running events. For more information or to enter, visit *www.runcyb.com*

WHAT NEXT? Try the Silver Trail Half Marathon route in Bwlch Nant yr Arian, near Aberystwyth. You might also enjoy waymarked trail runs at Newborough Forest on Ynys Môn (Anglesey); Tan y Coed near Machynlleth; or the Spirit of Llynfi Woodland near Maesteg. Elsewhere try Whinlatter Forest in the Lake District; Dalby Forest in North Yorkshire; Cannock Chase Forest in Staffordshire; and Kielder Forest in Northumberland.

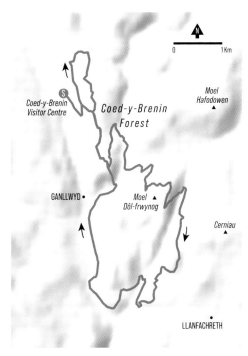

91
LLANGOLLEN FELL RACE

27km | **FELL** | **NAVIGATION** 1 fully waymarked
DENBIGHSHIRE

A long runnable race on fells and trails, enjoying beautiful views across Eglwyseg and Rhuabon mountains, and touching upon both Offa's Dyke Path and the World's End Trail to finish.

DISTANCE **27km**   ASCENT **640m**   TIME **3:00–4:30 hours**   RECORDS
(F) Catrin Smith 2:22.13 in 2022; (M) Tom Adams 1:49.42 in 2022
START/FINISH **Recreation ground to the north of Ysgol Dinas Bran, Llangollen**   GRID REF **SJ 214 424**   GPS **52.9731, -3.1719**   PUBLIC TRANSPORT **Llangollen has good bus links with surrounding towns and villages**   PARKING **Several car parks south of the river in Llangollen (parking charges apply)**

The understated tourist town of Llangollen is part of a UNESCO World Heritage Site which covers 18 kilometres of the Llangollen Canal (from Gledrid to the Horseshoe Falls, via the spectacular Pontcysyllte Aqueduct). Llangollen Fell Race was added to the racing calendar in 2019 and immediately proved popular on account of its enjoyable course and beautiful views across the Dee Valley around Llangollen.

The route has wonderful views, visiting the limestone escarpment of Trevor Rocks, the undulating heights of Eglwyseg Mountain, the steep incut valleys above World's End Farm and the summit of Cyrn-y-Brain with its two notable radio masts and the ruins of Sir Watkin's Tower, built as a folly in the 18th century. Sections of the route follow the beautiful World's End Trail and Offa's Dyke Path, and it is very runnable throughout.

OTHER OPTIONS   The race takes a figure-of-eight route, therefore it's possible to miss out the northern loop by cutting across to the return journey at the crossover point above World's End Farm. Just don't do this on race day!

RACE   The Run Free Fell Runners club organise a longer 27-kilometre and shorter 16-kilometre race (just the southern loop of the main race), *www.llangollenfellrace.co.uk*

WHAT NEXT?   For other similar trails in Wales try the Preseli Hills (see page 124); the Waun Fach Horseshoe in the Brecon Beacons; Abergavenny Three Peaks (see page 152); or the Berwyn Hills (see page 134). Elsewhere in Great Britain, try Nine Standards Rigg in the North Pennines (see page 14); the Scald Hill, Cheviot and Hedgehope Hill round in the Cheviots; the Sedbergh Hills Fell Race in Cumbria; the Ladybower Reservoir and Crook Hill loop in the Peak District; or the Ochil 2000s near Stirling (see page 92). For bigger summits head for the remote Arrochar Alps in Argyll and Bute or the Etive Hills south of Glen Coe in Scotland.

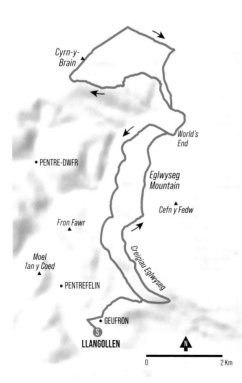

92

SEDBURY CLIFFS TO MONMOUTH

29km | TRAIL | NAVIGATION 1 *fully waymarked*
WALES–ENGLAND BORDER

This route covers the southern section of the fascinating Offa's Dyke Path National Trail, following an ancient earthwork which marked the border between Wales and England.

DISTANCE **29km** ASCENT **940m** TIME **3:00-4:45 hours**
START **Sedbury Cliffs, east of Cas-Gwent (Chepstow)**
FINISH **Monmouth** GRID REF **ST 552 928/SO 511 127** GPS **51.6326, -2.6484/51.8115, -2.7103** PUBLIC TRANSPORT **Regular buses run between Monmouth and Chepstow** PARKING **Several car parks in Sedbury and Chepstow – parking charges apply**

The historic Offa's Dyke Path is named after the extravagant dyke that King Offa ordered to be constructed in the 8th century which divided Offa's kingdom, Mercia, from rival kingdoms in what is now Wales, and which the trail often follows. It links three National Landscapes (the Wye Valley; the Shropshire Hills; and the Clwydian Range and Dee Valley) and is well waymarked throughout. This route covers the most southern section, running from Sedbury Cliffs along the picturesque Wye Valley to Monmouth.

The official start of the Offa's Dyke Path is the famous Sedbury Cliffs, overlooking the Severn Estuary; the trail then swings inland towards the Afon Gwy (River Wye). There are many great vantage points along this famous section of trail, including the Devil's

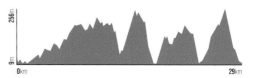

© KATE WORTHINGTON

Pulpit, where you can look over the Afon Gwy to ancient Tintern Abbey. Other highlights include the village of Brockweir, Cadora Woods Nature Reserve and the final viewpoint at the top of Kymin Hill. From here it's downhill into woodland and along tarmac lanes into Monmouth, nestled in the tranquil lower reaches of the Wye Valley.

OTHER OPTIONS The official Offa's Dyke Path website offers a vast amount of information on all sections, as well as suggested circular and linear routes along its length, *www.nationaltrail.co.uk/en_GB/trails/offas-dyke-path*

A related challenge is the King Offa's Sea to Summit route (35 kilometres with 1,340 metres of ascent) which follows Offa's Dyke Path from Prestatyn on the north coast of Wales to the summit of Moel Famau (finishing just beyond, at the car park at Bwlch Pen Barras).

ULTRA ROUTE The full Offa's Dyke Path is a 285-kilometre National Trail that links Sedbury Cliffs with Prestatyn;

it accrues approximately 7,500 metres of ascent. The FKT is held by Robin Smith (M), who covered the route in 3 days, 1 hour and 25 minutes in 2020.

RACE The King Offa's Dyke Race traverses the full length of the National Trail (with some slight deviations for checkpoints) and is organised by Beyond Marathon. There is also a 161-kilometre event called the Mercian Challenge. For further details or to enter, visit *www.kingoffasdyke.co.uk*

WHAT NEXT? For hilly sections, run the Offa's Dkye Path through the Brecon Beacons or the Clwydian Range in Denbighshire. If you prefer flatter trails, follow the route along the Afon Gwy and the Montgomery Canal. To race something similar, try the Llangollen Fell Race (see page 146) or Preseli Beast race routes (see page 124). Alternative long-distance trails include the Pennine Way, Southern Upland Way and West Highland Way.

93

YNYS GYBI (HOLY ISLAND)

43km | **TRAIL** | **NAVIGATION 1** fully waymarked
YNYS MÔN/ANGLESEY

A varied loop showcasing the quality and character of the stunning Isle of Anglesey Coastal Path.

DISTANCE **43km** ASCENT **440m** TIME **4-6 hours** START/FINISH **Penrhos Country Park, Holyhead** GRID REF **SH 274 805** GPS **53.2932, -4.5910** PUBLIC TRANSPORT **Penrhos Country Park has regular bus links to Holyhead, which has good onward bus and rail connections** PARKING **Penrhos Country Park car park (free)**

The Isle of Anglesey (Ynys Môn) – Wales's largest island – is separated from the Welsh mainland by the Menai Strait, which is spanned by two iconic bridges, the Menai Suspension Bridge and Pont Britannia. This challenge is an aesthetically pleasing loop (within the Anglesey Coastal Path), which traverses the whole coastline of Ynys Gybi, a smaller island off Ynys Môn.

Throughout the journey, the coastline will always be on your right! From the country park, the coastal path is well waymarked around the island and first visits the headland to your left (Gorsedd-y-penrhyn), then crosses Penrhos Beach and over the inner harbour of Holyhead port.

As you enter Holyhead Breakwater Country Park and the South Stack Cliffs Nature Reserve, the landscape changes to rugged coastline and cliffs. The trail hugs the edge of the island between North Stack and South Stack, along Gogarth Bay. Beyond the lighthouse at South Stack, the route continues south, sometimes heading inland on quiet lanes or through fields to regain the coast at another point. There are numerous tiny coves and inlets to spy from above. The next open stretch of beach is at Trearddur Bay. From here, enjoy rolling farmland, clifftops and coves before the route heads across more lovely beaches at Borthwen and Traeth Llydan (Silver Bay). Eventually the route makes a distinct turn north-west, heading

cross-country towards Four Mile Bridge, where the Inland Sea can be crossed by road. To close the loop, cross the Stanley Embankment on the A5 and head back to Penrhos Country Park.

OTHER OPTIONS If you need to cut the route short, use the network of small roads bisecting the island to cut back towards Penrhos Country Park. For shorter adventures in the area, try the nearby Holyhead Mountain Circular (8.2 kilometres with 280 metres of ascent) or the Newborough Beach and Ynys Llanddwyn loop (6.1 kilometres with 50 metres of ascent).

ULTRA ROUTE The full Isle of Anglesey Coastal Path follows much of Ynys Môn's undulating coastline, passing tiny coves, dramatic cliffs, farmland and coastal villages over a total distance of 219 kilometres, with 2,070 metres of ascent. It also forms part of the longer Wales Coast Path, a 1,400-kilometre long-distance walking route around the whole coast of Wales.

RACE The Ring O' Fire ultra follows the full Isle of Anglesey Coastal Path. For more information or to enter, visit *www.ringofire.co.uk*

WHAT NEXT? The Welsh coastline is rich in fantastic trail running. Check out the Gower coastline or Pembrokeshire Coast Path. Outside Wales, try an Isle of Portland loop (see page 12), the Jurassic Coast and other sections of the South West Coast Path. If you want to run further north, head to Scotland for the Fife Coastal Path or Moray Coast Trail.

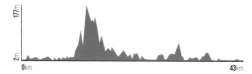

© JOHN COEFIELD

94

ABERGAVENNY THREE PEAKS

33km | FELL | NAVIGATION 3 no waymarking
THE BLACK MOUNTAINS

A demanding circular route in the Black Mountains, linking the summits of Blorens (Blorenge), Y Fâl (Sugar Loaf) and Ysgyryd Fawr (Skirrid), and clocking up some considerable vert!

DISTANCE **33km** ASCENT **1,340m** TIME **4–6 hours** RECORDS
**Unsupported: (F) Therese Woodier and Jade Williams 5:06.11 in 2019;
(M) Liam Glen 3:02.32 in 2021** START/FINISH **Abergavenny Scout Hall**
GRID REF **SO 299 145** GPS **51.8251, -3.0172** PUBLIC TRANSPORT
**Abergavenny has good bus and rail links with surrounding towns
and villages** PARKING **Fairfield car park, Abergavenny (parking
charges apply)**

BOTH PHOTOS © JOHN COEFIELD

This challenge was devised as a charity event by Chris Barber and first held in March 1963 – making it one of the oldest endurance events in the UK. Although originally aimed at walkers, it has since become popular with trail runners looking to test their mettle. There's now a choice of three other routes as the event continues to evolve, but the original – now known as the Gold Route – remains a classic.

In 1975 the start was moved from Crickhowell (from where entrants had a choice of whether to walk the route clockwise or anticlockwise) to Abergavenny, reducing the amount of road walking. The eponymous three peaks are Blorens (561 metres), Y Fâl (596 metres) and Ysgyryd Fawr (486 metres), which is topped by the remains of St Michael's Chapel.

The challenge attracts a wide range of human and canine participants. The youngest person to complete the route was a lad of seven, the son of Neville Tandy, the organiser of the Reservoir Roundabout (another excellent running challenge) and the Mid Wales Marathon.

OTHER OPTIONS The charity challenge event also offers a Platinum Route (shorter and steeper), a Silver Route (two of the three peaks) and a Bronze Route (a circular route over Y Fâl only). For full details visit *www.threepeakstrial.co.uk*

Many of these routes also cross the Beacons Way, a 159-kilometre long-distance trail from Abergavenny to Llangadog.

RACE Fell races in the surrounding area include Sugar Loaf (see page 128). The Black Mountains Fell Race is a longer route, starting from nearby village Llanbedr.

WHAT NEXT? For a full feast in the Black Mountains, there is a lockdown-inspired Rownd Mynydd Du (Black Mountains Round), which bags most hills in the range starting and finishing in Abergavenny. The route is 117 kilometres long with 5,260 metres of ascent. It was devised and later completed by local fell runner Brett Mahoney (with Tim Woodier) in 2021.

For similar routes across Great Britain try the Brecon Beacon Horseshoe; a round of the Duddon Valley, the Caldbeck Fells, Mosedale Fells or George Fisher's Tea Round in the Lake District (see page 38); the Chevy Chase in Northumberland (see page 29); or Ben Hope (see page 66) and Ben Loyal in the North West Highlands.

95

WELSH 1000m PEAKS RACE

33km | MOUNTAIN | NAVIGATION 4 difficult self-navigation or complex terrain
ERYRI/SNOWDONIA

Navigate over iconic ridges and summits to link all five of the 1,000-metre peaks in Eryri, finishing on the summit of Yr Wyddfa.

DISTANCE **33km** ASCENT **2,870m** TIME **5:30–7:30 hours**
RECORDS **(F)** T. Strain 4:33.28 in 2019; **(M)** J. Woods 04:02.38 in 2017 START **Abergwyngregyn** FINISH **Summit of Yr Wyddfa**
GRID REF **SH 647 731/SH 609 543** GPS **53.2376, -4.0276/53.0685, -4.0761**
PUBLIC TRANSPORT **Race bus ferries competitors from Llanberis to the start. To travel by public bus within the area visit www.traveline. cymru or www.sherparwyddfa.wales** PARKING **Limited parking (free) in Abergwyngregyn village. Competitors can park in Llanberis and catch the race bus**

First formally devised as an Army event in the 1950s, this peak-bagging challenge was later amended and opened to all in the 1960s. The first race took place in 1971, with various classes for mountaineers and fell runners. The event is also known as the Snowdonia Summits Marathon.

As a traditional fell race, route choice between checkpoints is down to the individual competitor. Runners start out along the road from Abergwyngregyn, following the Afon Rhaeadr-fawr to Aber Falls before striking out across the open fell to Yr Aryg. The first 1,000-metre peak is Carnedd Llewelyn and then Carnedd Dafydd, which is bagged as an out-and-back. Runners track back along Cefn Ysgolion Duon to reach the derelict wall checkpoint (grid reference: SH 676 631) before descending south to the Ogwen Valley Mountain Rescue Centre.

Competitors must turn right along the A5 and cross at the marshalled point to head up to the base of Y Gribin. Here the route climbs the Gribin Ridge to gain the summit of Glyder Fawr. A direct descent leads to the youth hostel at Pen-y-Pass, where runners join the popular Pyg Track. At the top, competitors must briefly tag the summit of Garnedd Ugain and about-turn before beginning the final climb up to the finish on the summit of Yr Wyddfa.

GOOD TO KNOW GPS devices are not permitted. The race map provided is marked with checkpoints only. The course is very technical and ascends the Gribin Ridge, which is waymarked on race day (grade-1 scramble).

OTHER OPTIONS There is also a shorter course linking three of the 1,000-metre summits. It starts at Ogwen Cottage and goes via the summit of Glyder Fawr, Pen-y-Pass and the summit of Garnedd Ugain –

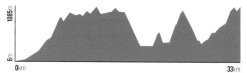

also finishing on the summit of Yr Wyddfa (13 kilometres with 1,550 metres of ascent).

RACE For more information on the race and to enter, visit *www.welsh1000m.org*

WHAT NEXT? A local alternative that also summits Snowdon is the Ras Pedol Peris. For Lake District fell races with classic status, try the Borrowdale Fell Race or the Great Lakes Fell Race, both of which tackle rocky terrain and take in England's highest mountain, Scafell Pike. The best Scottish equivalent is probably the iconic Isle of Jura Fell Race (see page 78).

96
WELSH 3000s

38km | MOUNTAIN | NAVIGATION 4 difficult self-navigation or complex terrain
ERYRI/SNOWDONIA

A classic, high-mountain challenge linking all summits over 3,000 feet in Eryri and visiting three distinctly different mountain ranges.

So old is this challenge, that it is not known who first succeeded in making the traverse, but it is recorded that Eustace Thomas of the Rucksack Club completed it in 1919 with friends. In a widely publicised record attempt in 1938, a second new record was set. But the major breakthrough came in the 1950s with the advent of mountain running (which caused much controversy at the time). In 1988, Colin Donnelly set a historic record which knocked 10 minutes off the great Joss Naylor's time, which had already become the stuff of Welsh legend. This record (4 hours and 19 minutes) stood for a further 31 years but was finally broken by Finlay Wild in 2019.

The pedigree of the women's record is less well-documented, but Angela Carson's impressive time of 1989 still stands.

But for many this challenge is not about breaking speed records, or any records in fact. The objective is instead to weave an intricate line that wanders through three enigmatic mountain ranges of Eryri in a singular outing. Following in the footsteps of early 20th-century walkers, runners seek to make the same fascinating journey for themselves; each mountain range offering up different adventure and character. Whatever the motivation, the journey is the same.

The massif of Yr Wyddfa, the stony Glyderau and the plateau of the Carneddau are all laid out ahead, spilling north to the coast like a wrinkled carpet; exciting, steep and slightly foreboding. Patience and planning will advantage the experienced runner, holding out for an opportunity with longer daylight hours and extended spells of settled weather, to aid

DISTANCE **approximately 38km** ASCENT **3,500m** TIME **7–12 hours**
RECORDS **(F) Angela Carson 5:28.21 in 1989; (M) Finlay Wild 4:10.48 in 2019**
START/FINISH **Most do the Yr Wyddfa massif first, starting either from Pen-y-Pass or the summit of Yr Wyddfa itself** GRID REF **SH 647 556 (start at Pen-y-Pass); SH 609 543 (start at Yr Wyddfa); SH 720 715 (finish)** GPS **53.0804, -4.0213 (start at Pen-y-Pass); 53.0685, -4.0761 (start at Yr Wyddfa); 53.2254, -3.9179 (finish)** PUBLIC TRANSPORT **Sherpa'r Wyddfa buses stop at Pen-y-Pass, www.sherparwyddfa.wales** PARKING **Pen-y-Pass car park (parking charges apply) operates a pre-booking system in high season – it is very busy and often full. Alternatives include a parking lay-by near Llyn Pen-y-Gwryd (parking charges apply) or Nant Peris Park and Ride**

progress and efficiency of pace over complex and ever-changing terrain. Some opt to bivvy up on Yr Wyddfa's summit before bagging Garnedd Ugain and the summit of Crib Goch, then descend into the Llanberis Pass. Runners will next ascend steeply from Nant Peris to tick off the five summits on the spiky Glyderau range, before dropping once more into the beautiful Ogwen Valley. The final range of the challenge is the the Carneddau – steep and rocky at first, these bulky summits become grassier and undulating as the route travels north. The Welsh 3000s challenge is a journey that overpays whatever you invest.

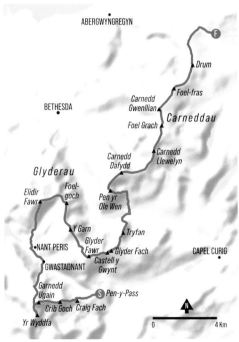

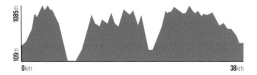

OTHER OPTIONS Challengers can choose any route and summit the mountains in any order. Some are seeking the fastest or most direct route, while others want to climb the mountain by the most aesthetic line.

RACE The Welsh 1000m Peaks Race (see page 154) takes a different route through similar terrain. Much of the Welsh 3000s route is also included in the first day of the infamous Dragon's Back Race. There are many traditional fell races on the peaks included in this challenge route. For a full listing of Welsh fell races visit the Welsh Fell Runners Association's race calendar: *www.wfra.org.uk/races*

WHAT NEXT? Other peak-bagging journeys of note include the Cairngorm 4000s (see page 108) and the Munro 24-hour round in Scotland; along with the Old County Tops Fell Race (see page 40), Steve Parr Round (Lakes 2500s), Lakes 24-hour round and the enormous Wainwrights Round in the Lake District. There are many other less well-known peak-bagging rounds across upland areas of Great Britain and plenty more waiting to be created!

97

SOUTH WALES TRAVERSE

117km | FELL | NAVIGATION 4 difficult self-navigation
or complex terrain
BRECON BEACONS

A linear, long-distance fell-running route
bagging 31 summits over 2,000 feet in the
Brecon Beacons.

DISTANCE **approximately 117km** ASCENT **5,100m** TIME **19–24 hours**
RECORDS **(F) Helen Brown in 18:48.45 in 2020; (M) Damian Hall 14:13.18
in 2020** START **Pen Rhiw-wen** FINISH **Llanthony Priory** GRID REF
SN 730 184/SO 289 278 GPS **51.8497, -3.8452/51.9441, -3.0357**
PUBLIC TRANSPORT **No practical options** PARKING **Car parks (free)
are available at the start (A4069, Pen Rhiw-wen) and end (Llanthony
Priory) of the route** MORE INFO **If you complete in under 24 hours,
you can be added to the completions log**

Originally known as the Brecon Beacons Traverse, this
challenge was established in 1984 by Derek Fisher
and Andy Lewsley, who had completed it in 1983
in 21 hours and 24 minutes. It is a true linear, long-
distance challenge that crosses the mountain ranges
of the Black Mountain, Carmarthenshire Fans, Fforest
Fawr, Central Brecon Beacons, the Black Mountains,
as well as most of the Brecon Beacons National Park.
What better way to discover the high points of South

Wales than to link them all together in one continuous
outing? It can be completed in either direction.

If starting in the west, begin at Pen Rhiw-wen – the
highest point of the A4069 – and follow the Beacons
Way towards Fan Brycheiniog, before dropping down to
road level again. Wonderful grassy fell running follows
(though some climbs are very steep!) to the Storey
Arms Centre, at the foot of Pen y Fan. Well-engineered
tourist trails make the going slightly easier over the

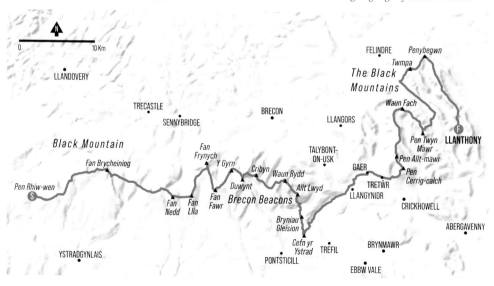

well-known Brecon Beacon summits of Corn Du, Pen y Fan and Cribyn, although the relentless ascent and descent is wearing. There is some fantastic upland running to the east of the Brecon Beacons, as the fierce undulations ease a little. Beware the loss of height down to Talybont Reservoir, before climbing again to 617 metres – only to descend (mostly on road) to the Afon Wysg (River Usk)! Your knees will thank you, however, as you return to soft ground, heading into the Black Mountains for an expansive loop. Next you graze the Wales–England border for a time along Offa's Dyke Path, before finally coming to a stop in the village of Llanthony, in the secluded Vale of Ewyas.

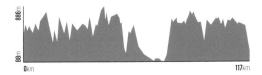

OTHER OPTIONS There are multiple road crossings for meeting your crew or to break the route into a multi-day journey (transport support required). It can also be broken at Brecon to give a nice two-day option.

RACE For shorter fell running routes in the Brecon Beacon National Park try the Cribyn Fell Race or the Brecon Fans Races – two great horseshoes on consecutive days, *www.breconfans.org.uk* Ultras in the region include the Beacons Way Ultra (*www.gbultras.com/beacons-way-ultra-100*) and day five of the infamous Dragon's Back Race.

WHAT NEXT? For similar challenges try the shorter Cumbrian Traverse (see page 42), sections of the Offa's Dyke Path, the Southern Upland Way, the Cambrian Way or the Pennine Way.

98

LLWYBR LLECHI ERYRI/ SNOWDONIA SLATE TRAIL

134km | TRAIL | NAVIGATION 1 fully waymarked
ERYRI/SNOWDONIA

Journey through time, linking the historic mining villages and unique slate landscapes of North Wales's newest World Heritage Site.

DISTANCE **134km** ASCENT **3,400m** TIME **25–30 hours**
RECORDS **(F) Nikki Sommers 25:32.00 in 2020; (M) Connaire Cann 21:52.00 in 2023** START **Porth Penrhyn, Bangor** FINISH **Bethesda**
GRID REF **SH 592 728/SH 623 666** GPS **53.2335, -4.1109/53.1793, -4.0611**
PUBLIC TRANSPORT **To travel between villages along the route by bus visit www.traveline.cymru or www.sherparwyddfa.wales**
PARKING **There is limited parking at Porth Penrhyn, suitable for drop-off only. Long-term parking is available in Bangor** MORE INFO **www.snowdoniaslatetrail.org**

The Snowdonia Slate Trail is a seductive concept: a 134-kilometre multi-stage sightseeing tour in Eryri, linking popular sights with hidden gems. First conceived by local Aled Owen and opened in 2017, the 13 sections can be followed as a continuous journey, over multiple days or over several visits – it's an expedition to savour!

The creative route weaves together existing paths and tracks through woodland, valleys, upland, heath, abandoned quarries and diverse villages. There is an ever-present reference to this area's close relationship with the bedrock of the surrounding mountains. Runners are reminded of the abundant slate quarrying history and communities that thrived here to the hustle of slate wagons and railways, as workers young and old chipped away at huge slate walls with rudimentary tools.

Running anticlockwise from Bangor, the trail visits the villages of Bethesda, Llanberis, Waunfawr, Beddgelert, Blaenau Ffestiniog, Betws-y-Coed and Capel Curig on its journey – threading together quiet trails with busier public footpaths, lanes and bridleways. Remarkably the route visits five historic narrow-gauge railways: the Penrhyn Quarry Railway, the Llanberis Lake Railway, the Snowdon Mountain Railway, the Welsh Highland Light Railway and the Ffestiniog Railway!

Collect eight stamps in your official trail passport from designated venues along the way to earn yourself a commemorative medal.

OTHER OPTIONS You can split this journey into a number of days or you can run sections as separate linear routes. There is a phenomenal amount of information available from the official website about all 13 sections and also about surrounding trails.

RACE Apex Running have two events on this fascinating trail – the 88-kilometre Ultra Tour of the Quarries, or the Slate Trail Ultra, which covers the whole trail, *www.apexrunning.co*

WHAT NEXT? For a more mountainous journey, try the South Wales Traverse (see page 158). Similar historic trails elsewhere in Great Britain include Hadrian's Wall Path, John Muir Way, Cotswold Way, The Ridgeway or sections of the Offa's Dyke Path.

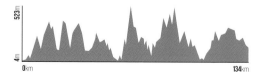

© SHUTTERSTOCK/GAIL JOHNSON

Ynys Môn/
Anglesey

Menai Strait

S **PORTH PENRHYN**

MENAI BRIDGE
BANGOR
• ABERGWYNGREGYN
LLANDYGAI
• TAL-Y-BONT
LLANLLECHID

COED-Y-PARC • **F** **BETHESDA**

CAERNARFON
GALLT-Y-FOEL
DINORWIG
LLANBERIS
WAUNFAWR
Llyn Peris

Pen yr
Ole Wen ▲

• LLANRWST

Glyderau

RHOSGADFAN
Llyn Cwellyn
Glyder Fawr ▲
CAPEL CURIG
BETWS-Y-COED

Y FRON
Yr Wyddfa ▲
NANTLLE
Yr Wyddfa
Range
DOLWYDDELAN

TALYSARN •
RHYD-DDU
PENMACHNO

BEDDGELERT
Moelwynion

BLAENAU
FFESTINIOG
CWM PENMACHNO

NANTMOR
TANYGRISIAU

CROESOR
LLAN FFESTINIOG

N

0   10 Km

BONT NEWYDD

99
PADDY BUCKLEY ROUND

104km | **FELL** | **NAVIGATION 4** difficult self-navigation
or complex terrain
ERYRI/SNOWDONIA

The Welsh answer to the Bob Graham Round
is arguably the toughest of Great Britain's
'Big Three' mountain rounds. Rough terrain
and tricky navigation make this a hard-earned
classic.

DISTANCE **104km** ASCENT **7,260m** TIME **24–36 hours**
RECORDS **(F) Lizzie Richardson 17:22.54 in 2023; (M) Finlay Wild
15:14.45 in 2022** START/FINISH **Capel Curig** GRID REF **SH 720 582**
GPS **53.1058, -3.9130** PUBLIC TRANSPORT **To travel around Eryri
by bus visit www.traveline.cymru or www.sherparwyddfa.wales**
PARKING **Capel Curig car park (free)** MORE INFO **While we've listed
the start as Capel Curig, the round may be started at any point and
can be completed in either direction**

Paddy Buckley's 'Welsh Classical' round was conceived
in 1977 to 1978 – with input from Chris Brasher
and members of the Rucksack Club – as a Welsh
equivalent to the Lake District's Bob Graham Round
and to showcase the Welsh hills he loved. It takes in
47 summits in Eryri, including Yr Wyddfa (Snowdon).
The route traverses the well-known high mountain
ranges of Yr Wyddfa, the Glyderau and the Carneddau
as well as the slightly less visited ranges of Moel Siabod,
the Moelwynion, Moel Hebog and the Nantlle Ridge.

It was first completed in 1982 by Wendy Dodds in
25 hours and 35 minutes; the first sub-24-hour round
was completed in 1985 by Martin Stone (23 hours
and 26 minutes) and fell-running legends Lizzie
Richardson and Finlay Wild hold the current records
for women and men, respectively.

Unlike the Bob Graham Round, the Paddy Buckley
Round doesn't need to be completed within 24 hours to
be considered a 'completion' – it just has to be done in
one continuous push (although many people will aim
to complete it in under 24 hours). There are no rules
about how it should be attempted, and completions are
recorded by Paddy Buckley himself. While Capel Curig
forms a logical start and finish point for the round, it can
actually be started anywhere along the route and be completed in either a clockwise or anticlockwise direction.

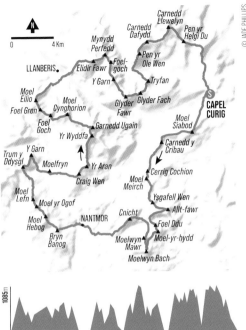

OTHER OPTIONS The round naturally breaks into five distinct legs, which start and finish where the route meets roads; these make for excellent shorter challenges in their own right. Going clockwise: Capel Curig to Nantmor (leg 1), Nantmor to Pont Cae Gors (leg 2), Pont Cae Gors (via Yr Wyddfa) to Llanberis (leg 3), Llanberis to Llyn Ogwen (leg 4) and finally Llyn Ogwen to Capel Curig (leg 5).

RACE As with all classic long rounds, this route takes in several summits that are part of established fell races, including Yr Wyddfa, Moel Hebog, Moel Siabod and Moelwyn Mawr. There are a number of ultras too, including the Yr Wyddfa Ultra 100 and Yr Wyddfa Ultra 50 from GB Ultras, *www.gbultras.com*, and the Ultra Trail Snowdonia/Eryri series from UTMB, *snowdonia.utmb.world*

WHAT NEXT? The Paddy Buckley Round is one of Great Britain's 'Big Three' mountain rounds, so the other two rounds – the Bob Graham Round (see page 48) and the Charlie Ramsay Round (see page 114) – are natural next steps. An alternative within Wales would be the more southerly Meirionnydd Round (see page 124) or, for a shorter introduction to North Wales, consider the Welsh 3000s (see page 156).

100
CAMBRIAN WAY

479km | FELL | NAVIGATION 2 partial waymarking
WALES

Wales's most diverse, challenging and scenically beautiful long-distance route between the north and south coasts.

DISTANCE **479km** ASCENT **22,500m** TIME **6–21 days** RECORDS **(M) Seth Kennard 6:14:07.00 in 2021** START **Cardiff Castle** FINISH **Conwy Castle** GRID REF **ST 180 764/SH 783 774** GPS **51.4810, -3.1820/53.2800, -3.8255** PUBLIC TRANSPORT **Good bus and rail links at the start and finish, www.traveline.cymru** MORE INFO **If walking south to north, the prevailing wind direction should be mostly (though not always) behind you**

Described as the Mountain Connoisseur's trail, the route quickly leaves the bustle of Cardiff behind and follows the well-marked Taff Trail, before swinging north-east towards Pontypool and then north to complete a loop around the Black Mountains. On paper, the route may seem a little incongruous here, but there are many upland areas of Wales to explore, and the journey would not be doing justice to Wales's diverse landscapes if it did not pay a visit! Once completed, the Cambrian Way heads back west to cover the entire Brecon Beacons range and on to the Black Mountain area, south of Llandovery. This area packs a punch in terms of ascent, descent and reascent! From Llandovery, the route progresses north through remote Mid Wales and Pen Pumlumon, and on to Dinas Mawddwy.

A swing west visits Cadair Idris and the coast at Barmouth, before exploring another wild section over the wonderful Rhinogydd mountains. This last section may take longer than planned, as the ground is quite rough underfoot. North of the Rhinogydd range are the quiet hills of the Moelwynion area of Eryri, which are a tonic to the more frequented routes of northern Eryri. The Cambrian Way takes in the highlights of Yr Wyddfa and the gloriously rocky Glyderau mountain summits, before it takes on the final range of mountains in the north of Wales; the backbone of the Carneddau. As the high Carneddau summits give way to heather-clad foothills towards Wales's north coast, the route finally comes to rest in Conwy.

GOOD TO KNOW The Cambrian Way Trust official website is a source of endless information on the route and the history of its development, as well as providing links to GPX files, maps and guidebooks, *www.cambrianway. org.uk*

Along the Way there is increasing waymarking of lowland sections but the mountainous areas remain unwaymarked (self-navigation required here).

OTHER OPTIONS For a shorter challenge, sections of the Cambrian Way can be tackled on their own.

RACE The Dragon's Back Race also traverses Wales, crossing the same mountains as the Cambrian Way but via an alternative line, determined largely by the runners (who are only required to visit the designated checkpoints along the way). *www.dragonsbackrace.com*

WHAT NEXT? If you have loved this epic mountain journey, you might also enjoy the Pennine Way or Cape Wrath Trail.

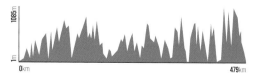

Ynys Môn/
Anglesey
BANGOR
CONWY
CHESTER
Carneddau
Glyderau
WREXHAM
Yr Wyddfa
Moelwynion
Eryri
Y BALA
Rhinogydd
BARMOUTH
DOLGELLAU
Cadair
Idris
Pumlumon
Fawr
ABERYSTWYTH
RHAYADER
TREGARON
The Black
Mountains
LLANDOVERY
CRICKHOWELL
The Black
Mountain
ABERGAVENNY
Fforest
Brecon
Fawr
Beacons
PONTYPOOL
PORT TALBOT
CAERPHILLY
RISCA
CARDIFF

N

0   40 Km

Appendix

Routes and inspiration

www.walkhighlands.co.uk
www.nationaltrail.co.uk
www.scotlandsgreattrails.com
www.stevenfallon.co.uk
www.ukhillwalking.com/logbook/r/find.php
www.alltrails.com
www.munromagic.com
www.themunrosociety.com
www.forestryengland.uk/running
runtogether.co.uk/routes
www.britishorienteering.org.uk
www.nationaltrust.org.uk/visit/outdoor-activities
www.fionaoutdoors.co.uk

FKTs

www.gofar.org.uk
www.bobgrahamclub.org.uk
fastestknowntime.com
www.gomountaingoats.com/fkt
www.scottishhillrunners.uk/LongDistance.aspx

Races

www.fellrunner.org.uk
www.wfra.org.uk
www.scottishhillrunners.uk
www.sientries.co.uk
www.parkrun.org.uk

Weather

www.mwis.org.uk
www.metoffice.gov.uk

Mountaineering

www.thebmc.co.uk
www.mountaineering.scot

Winter skills courses

www.girlsonhills.com
*www.mountaineering.scot/safety-and-skills/courses-and-
    events/courses*
www.glenmorelodge.org.uk/winter-mountain

© DAVID MILLER

Acknowledgements

I am extremely grateful to all those who have contributed to this book by providing ideas, information and support – hopefully together we will have inspired many to take on new challenges and expand their experiences. Thank you specifically to Kate Worthington (Raw Adventures) for her significant input on the challenges in Wales, and to Virginia Bird and Rebecca Weeks for administrative support throughout. Thank you to Shane and Heather Ohly, Rob Greenwood, Nicky Spinks, Nicola Redgwell and Martyn Price for edits, suggestions and advice.

Thanks also go to all the race organisers of events referenced in this book and the organisations and individuals who act as custodians of the rounds and records that have kept generations of runners inspired and motivated. This includes all the curators and caretakers of the National Trails mentioned herein.

A huge thank you to all the photographers who have kindly allowed us to reproduce their images, including Pete Aylward, Jon Barton, Ross Brannigan, Donnie Campbell, John Coefield, Ken Douglas, Peter Ferguson, Barbara Fuller, Huw Gilbert, William Holyoak, Ross Jenkin, Rob Johnson, David Miller, Jonny Muir, Jade Phillips, Martyn Price, Kirsty Reade, Nicola Redgwell, Stephen Ross, Jamie Rutherford, Ewan Thorburn, Chris Upson, Paul Webster, Finlay Wild, Stephen Wilson and Kate Worthington.

This book has benefited enormously from the use of the Jones–Ross formula, used for calculating the timings associated with each challenge. Thank you to Kingsley Jones and Stephen Ross for this important component.

And finally, thank you to my family and to my Girls on Hills colleague Nancy Kennedy for the support and encouragement necessary for making ideas a reality.